MEGA HUGE

CN
CARTOON NETWORK™

MAD LIBS®

PSS!
PRICE STERN SLOAN
An Imprint of Penguin Random House

D1227869

PRICE STERN SLOAN
Penguin Young Readers Group
An Imprint of Penguin Random House LLC

Mad Libs format copyright © 2016 by Price Stern Sloan,
an imprint of Penguin Random House LLC. All rights reserved.

Concept created by Roger Price & Leonard Stern

Mega Huge Cartoon Network Mad Libs published in 2016 by Price Stern Sloan,
an imprint of Penguin Random House LLC, 345 Hudson Street, New York,
New York 10014. Printed in the USA.

Mega Huge Cartoon Network Mad Libs ISBN 9780399541384
1 3 5 7 9 10 8 6 4 2

PSS!
PRICE STERN SLOAN
An Imprint of Penguin Random House

MAD LIBS®

INSTRUCTIONS

MAD LIBS® is a game for people who don't like games!
It can be played by one, two, three, four, or forty.

• RIDICULOUSLY SIMPLE DIRECTIONS

In this tablet you will find stories containing blank spaces where words are left out. One player, the READER, selects one of these stories. The READER does not tell anyone what the story is about. Instead, he/she asks the other players, the WRITERS, to give him/her words. These words are used to fill in the blank spaces in the story.

• TO PLAY

The READER asks each WRITER in turn to call out a word—an adjective or a noun or whatever the space calls for—and uses them to fill in the blank spaces in the story. The result is a MAD LIBS® game.

When the READER then reads the completed MAD LIBS® game to the other players, they will discover that they have written a story that is fantastic, screamingly funny, shocking, silly, crazy, or just plain dumb—depending upon which words each WRITER called out.

• EXAMPLE (*Before* and *After*)

"_____!" he said _____
    EXCLAMATION   ADVERB

as he jumped into his convertible _____ and
                                NOUN

drove off with his _____ wife.
             ADJECTIVE

"_____OUCH_____!" he said _____STUPIDLY_____
    EXCLAMATION   ADVERB

as he jumped into his convertible _____CAT_____ and
                                NOUN

drove off with his _____BRAVE_____ wife.
             ADJECTIVE

QUICK REVIEW

In case you have forgotten what adjectives, adverbs, nouns, and verbs are, here is a quick review:

An ADJECTIVE describes something or somebody. *Lumpy, soft, ugly, messy,* and *short* are adjectives.

An ADVERB tells how something is done. It modifies a verb and usually ends in "ly." *Modestly, stupidly, greedily,* and *carefully* are adverbs.

A NOUN is the name of a person, place, or thing. *Sidewalk, umbrella, bridle, bathtub,* and *nose* are nouns.

A VERB is an action word. *Run, pitch, jump,* and *swim* are verbs. Put the verbs in past tense if the directions say PAST TENSE. *Ran, pitched, jumped,* and *swam* are verbs in the past tense.

When we ask for A PLACE, we mean any sort of place: a country or city *(Spain, Cleveland)* or a room *(bathroom, kitchen).*

An EXCLAMATION or SILLY WORD is any sort of funny sound, gasp, grunt, or outcry, like *Wow!, Ouch!, Whomp!, Ick!,* and *Gadzooks!*

When we ask for specific words, like a NUMBER, a COLOR, an ANIMAL, or a PART OF THE BODY, we mean a word that is one of those things, like *seven, blue, horse,* or *head.*

When we ask for a PLURAL, it means more than one. For example, *cat* pluralized is *cats.*

MAD LIBS® is fun to play with friends, but you can also play it by yourself! To begin with, DO NOT look at the story on the page below. Fill in the blanks on this page with the words called for. Then, using the words you have selected, fill in the blank spaces in the story.

Now you've created your own hilarious MAD LIBS® game!

ALL ABOUT
JAKE AND FINN

ANIMAL _____

PLURAL NOUN _____

VERB ENDING IN "ING" _____

ADJECTIVE _____

NOUN _____

NOUN _____

NOUN _____

ADJECTIVE _____

ADVERB _____

VERB _____

NOUN _____

ADJECTIVE _____

A PLACE _____

VERB ENDING IN "ING" _____

Jake the _____ and Finn the Human are not only best

ANIMAL

_____, they're also brothers. When Finn was a little baby,

PLURAL NOUN

Jake's parents found him in the woods _____ by himself.

VERB ENDING IN "ING"

Now the buddies live together in their way-_____ Tree Fort

ADJECTIVE

in the _____ Lands section of Ooo. While they may be as close

NOUN

as two peas in a/an _____, there are a few differences between

NOUN

them. Jake's got magical stretchy powers and can make himself as big as

a/an _____ or as _____ as a worm. While Jake gets

NOUN   ADJECTIVE

_____ sidetracked, Finn wants nothing more than to get up and

ADVERB

_____. With a cross-_____ and sword by his side,

VERB   NOUN

Finn is really _____ at taking down evil. Finn is superbrave and

ADJECTIVE

would go to the ends of (the) _____ to help anyone who is up

A PLACE

against bad vibes. One thing's for sure—both dudes are always down for

some adventure time and a gut-_____ laugh!

VERB ENDING IN "ING"

MAD LIBS® is fun to play with friends, but you can also play it by yourself! To begin with, DO NOT look at the story on the page below. Fill in the blanks on this page with the words called for. Then, using the words you have selected, fill in the blank spaces in the story.

Now you've created your own hilarious MAD LIBS® game!

JAKE THE ALMOST LUMPER, BY FINN

NOUN _____

VERB (PAST TENSE) _____

PART OF THE BODY _____

ADJECTIVE _____

PLURAL NOUN _____

VERB _____

ADJECTIVE _____

NOUN _____

PART OF THE BODY _____

VERB _____

ADVERB _____

EXCLAMATION _____

ADJECTIVE _____

ADJECTIVE _____

NUMBER _____

PLURAL NOUN _____

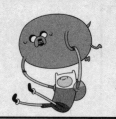

MAD LIBS
JAKE THE ALMOST LUMPER, BY FINN

This one time, Lumpy Space Princess accidentally bit Jake, and I was

all, "Holy _____ balls, bro! You're turning into a lumper!" Jake
　　　　　　NOUN

_____ into a full-on lump. His _____ got way-
VERB (PAST TENSE)　　　　　　　　　　　　　　　PART OF THE BODY

puffy. His voice got super-_____. His mood _____
　　　　　　　　　　　　　ADJECTIVE　　　　　　　　　　PLURAL NOUN

were stank. And worst of all, he blew me off to _____ at the
　　　　　　　　　　　　　　　　　　　　　　　　　VERB

Lumpy Prom. If I didn't save him from a/an _____ lifetime of
　　　　　　　　　　　　　　　　　　　ADJECTIVE

lump, no one would! I scored the cure from some lumpers who were using

it to keep their _____ as smooth as a baby's _____.
　　　　　　　　NOUN　　　　　　　　　　　　　　　PART OF THE BODY

Then I had them _____ me into a lumper with some bites so I
　　　　　　　　　VERB

could _____ float to the dance. There, Jake was all "_____!
　　　ADVERB　　　　　　　　　　　　　　　　　　　　EXCLAMATION

I don't want that lumping, _____ cure!" My memory is a little
　　　　　　　　　　　ADJECTIVE

_____ since my brain went _____ percent lump,
ADJECTIVE　　　　　　　　　　　　　　NUMBER

but somehow we both got back to normal. We celebrated by shaking our

_____ to groovy tunes. Epic win!
PLURAL NOUN

MAD LIBS® is fun to play with friends, but you can also play it by yourself! To begin with, DO NOT look at the story on the page below. Fill in the blanks on this page with the words called for. Then, using the words you have selected, fill in the blank spaces in the story.

Now you've created your own hilarious MAD LIBS® game!

WHY DON'T YOU LOVE ME, PRINCESSES EVERYWHERE?, BY ICE KING

ADJECTIVE _____

NOUN _____

PART OF THE BODY _____

EXCLAMATION _____

NOUN _____

ADJECTIVE _____

VERB ENDING IN "ING" _____

ADJECTIVE _____

NOUN _____

NOUN _____

VERB _____

PLURAL NOUN _____

NOUN _____

ADVERB _____

ADJECTIVE _____

NOUN _____

PLURAL NOUN _____

NOUN _____

"Hey, bro, why is it so _____ in here?" asked Pizza Steve as
_____ADJECTIVE_____

he rode in circles on his motorized speed _____. "I think the
_____NOUN_____

lightbulb _____," replied Mr. Gus. "_____ should
_____VERB (PAST TENSE)_____   _____PERSON IN ROOM_____

probably change it." "Hey, Uncle Grandpa, want to help me change a/an

_____?" asked Uncle Grandpa. "Sure, Uncle Grandpa," replied
____NOUN____

Uncle Grandpa as he popped up from a hole in the _____. "Just
_____NOUN_____

climb up on my _____." "Okay, Uncle Grandpa. I just
_____PART OF THE BODY_____

need to go to (the) _____ to get a new lightbulb first. What size
_____A PLACE_____

do we need?" "_____ watts," Uncle Grandpa replied. "I have one
_____NUMBER_____

of those," Belly Bag added. "Except that it's _____ and shaped
_____COLOR_____

like a/an _____." "Perfect," replied Uncle Grandpa. "Now all we
_____NOUN_____

need is _____ horses, a pack of strawberry _____, and
_____NUMBER_____   _____PLURAL NOUN_____

_____ to help screw it in."
____CELEBRITY____

MAD LIBS® is fun to play with friends, but you can also play it by yourself! To begin with, DO NOT look at the story on the page below. Fill in the blanks on this page with the words called for. Then, using the words you have selected, fill in the blank spaces in the story.

Now you've created your own hilarious MAD LIBS® game!

GIANT REALISTIC FLYING TIGER'S TIPS FOR TEENS

ADJECTIVE _____

NOUN _____

PLURAL NOUN _____

PERSON IN ROOM (MALE) _____

ADJECTIVE _____

PART OF THE BODY _____

PLURAL NOUN _____

NUMBER _____

PERSON IN ROOM _____

ADJECTIVE _____

COLOR _____

ARTICLE OF CLOTHING (PLURAL) _____

COLOR _____

PLURAL NOUN _____

MAD LIBS®
WHY DON'T YOU LOVE ME, PRINCESSES EVERYWHERE?, BY ICE KING

Dear _____ Princesses of Ooo,
      ADJECTIVE

What does a single _____ like me need to do to get a bride
                         NOUN

around here? I've racked my _____ thinking up ways to win
                              PART OF THE BODY

your love, but you keep saying "_____! Get away from me, you
                                   EXCLAMATION

psycho _____!" Is it my long, _____ beard that's
        NOUN   ADJECTIVE

scaring you? Because I tried _____ it off once, and you thought
                             VERB ENDING IN "ING"

I was too nice! Is it my pointy, _____ nose or my freezing, blue
                                   ADJECTIVE

_____? You shouldn't judge a/an _____ by its cover, you
    NOUN   NOUN

know. Sure, I may _____ you from your home and lock you up
                      VERB

behind steel _____ on occasion, but it's only because I want to tie
             PLURAL NOUN

the _____ and make you my _____ beloved wife! Is that
      NOUN   ADVERB

so wrong? How I wish to embrace you in a subzero, _____ hug!
                                                     ADJECTIVE

Princesses, can't you see I have a heart made of _____? I'd walk
                                                    NOUN

a million _____ to hypnotize you into saying "I do." It's just the
          PLURAL NOUN

kind of _____ I am.
          NOUN

MAD LIBS® is fun to play with friends, but you can also play it by yourself! To begin with, DO NOT look at the story on the page below. Fill in the blanks on this page with the words called for. Then, using the words you have selected, fill in the blank spaces in the story.

Now you've created your own hilarious MAD LIBS® game!

MY A+ APPLE PIE RECIPE, BY TREE TRUNKS

ADJECTIVE _____

NOUN _____

VERB _____

NOUN _____

ADJECTIVE _____

NUMBER _____

PLURAL NOUN _____

NOUN _____

COLOR _____

NOUN _____

NOUN _____

NUMBER _____

NOUN _____

ADJECTIVE _____

VERB ENDING IN "ING" _____

NOUN _____

PART OF THE BODY _____

COLOR _____

MAD LIBS®
MY A+ APPLE PIE RECIPE, BY TREE TRUNKS

Hi, y'all! Make a tasty, _____-fashioned apple pie with my
                                  ADJECTIVE

step-by-_____ recipe! First, go outside and _____
           NOUN   VERB

the freshest apples right from the branch. I use my long _____ to
                                                      NOUN

reach up high! There should be no rotten or _____ spots on your
                                                ADJECTIVE

apples. Each one must be _____ percent perfect! No ifs, ands, or
                                 NUMBER

_____ about it. Use a sharp _____ to carefully cut each
PLURAL NOUN   NOUN

apple into slices. Add 1 cup of _____ sugar, ¼ cup flour, and a
                                     COLOR

tea-_____ of cinnamon. Grab a wooden _____ and
        NOUN   NOUN

mix it all up! For the crust, combine _____ cups of flour, a pinch
                                     NUMBER

of _____, 1 cup of butter, and ½ cup of _____ water.
   NOUN   ADJECTIVE

Use a/an _____ pin to press the dough flat. Place the dough
        VERB ENDING IN "ING"

into a greased _____, then add the apples. Pop your pie into a
           NOUN

warm oven and keep a close _____ on it. When the crust turns
                       PART OF THE BODY

light _____, it's done!
    COLOR

From ADVENTURE TIME MAD LIBS® • ™ & © Cartoon Network. (s12). Published in 2012 by
Price Stern Sloan, an imprint of Penguin Random House LLC, 345 Hudson Street, New York, NY 10014.

MAD LIBS® is fun to play with friends, but you can also play it by yourself! To begin with, DO NOT look at the story on the page below. Fill in the blanks on this page with the words called for. Then, using the words you have selected, fill in the blank spaces in the story.

Now you've created your own hilarious MAD LIBS® game!

HOW TO HANDLE A CANDY ZOMBIE ATTACK, BY PRINCESS BUBBLEGUM

ADJECTIVE _____

NOUN _____

VERB ENDING IN "ING" _____

ADJECTIVE _____

PLURAL NOUN _____

TYPE OF LIQUID _____

PLURAL NOUN _____

PLURAL NOUN _____

ADJECTIVE _____

VERB _____

PLURAL NOUN _____

NOUN _____

Uh-oh! Did your plan to revive _____ Candy People result in
ADJECTIVE

zombification due to a malfunctioning decorpsinator serum? Go back to the

drawing _____ and correct the serum formula immediately! Remember:
NOUN

Candy Zombies go on a/an _____ frenzy when they're near
VERB ENDING IN "ING"

sugar. Round up a group of tried-and-_____ non-sugary friends
ADJECTIVE

to keep the zombies from attacking innocent _____. Spraying a
PLURAL NOUN

zombie with something sour, like pickle _____, will temporarily
TYPE OF LIQUID

stop them in their _____. Most likely, the zombies are after
PLURAL NOUN

one thing: Candy People! Candy People tend to explode into bits and

_____ when frightened, so keep the zombies a secret! Try this:
PLURAL NOUN

Tie a/an _____-fold around their eyes. Shout, "Piñata time!" and
ADJECTIVE

give each Candy Person a stick to _____ in the air. Soon the zombies
VERB

will be dropping like _____. And the best part? You can turn them
PLURAL NOUN

back into healthy _____ People once you've fixed the serum!
NOUN

Mathematical!

MAD LIBS® is fun to play with friends, but you can also play it by yourself! To begin with, DO NOT look at the story on the page below. Fill in the blanks on this page with the words called for. Then, using the words you have selected, fill in the blank spaces in the story.

Now you've created your own hilarious MAD LIBS® game!

SONG ABOUT OOO

VERB _____

ADJECTIVE _____

PART OF THE BODY (PLURAL) _____

NOUN _____

PLURAL NOUN _____

COLOR _____

ADJECTIVE _____

VERB ENDING IN "ING" _____

ADJECTIVE _____

NOUN _____

ANIMAL _____

EXCLAMATION _____

PART OF THE BODY _____

VERB ENDING IN "ING" _____

PLURAL NOUN _____

ADJECTIVE _____

NOUN _____

PART OF THE BODY _____

MAD LIBS

SONG ABOUT OOO

Help Marceline _____ the lyrics to her catchy,

VERB

_____ song about her special spots in Ooo!

ADJECTIVE

I'm way old, like over a thousand, and my _____ have seen

PART OF THE BODY (PLURAL)

so much stuff. No _____ about it, travelin's my habit, 'cause I

NOUN

can never get enough. I'm all aaah in Ooo! Like head over _____

PLURAL NOUN

for Ooo! Suckin' out the _____ from Strawberry Patch is the most

COLOR

_____ treat around. Love to thrash with my axe-bass. Tell me

ADJECTIVE

you're so _____ the sound. Ooo, my house is cozy, it's inside a

VERB ENDING IN "ING"

deep, _____ cave! Aaah, it's got a recording _____ plus

ADJECTIVE   NOUN

my zombie pet _____, who's my fave. I'm all _____

ANIMAL   EXCLAMATION

in Ooo! Like, _____ over heels for Ooo! Hula-_____

PART OF THE BODY   VERB ENDING IN "ING"

in the Fire Kingdom with hot _____ at my feet. Hangin' in

PLURAL NOUN

_____ Forest with the ghosties is sweet. Grasslands got my old

ADJECTIVE

pad, the _____ Fort. There's Finn and Jake who make my

NOUN

_____ totally snort. I'm way aaah for Ooo, yeahweeeooo!

PART OF THE BODY

From ADVENTURE TIME MAD LIBS® • ™ & © Cartoon Network. (s12). Published in 2012 by
Price Stern Sloan, an imprint of Penguin Random House LLC, 345 Hudson Street, New York, NY 10014.

MAD LIBS® is fun to play with friends, but you can also play it by yourself! To begin with, DO NOT look at the story on the page below. Fill in the blanks on this page with the words called for. Then, using the words you have selected, fill in the blank spaces in the story.

Now you've created your own hilarious MAD LIBS® game!

WHY I BECAME A MONSTER, BY LUMPY SPACE PRINCESS

NOUN _____

PLURAL NOUN _____

VERB ENDING IN "ING" _____

VERB _____

A PLACE _____

PLURAL NOUN _____

VERB _____

NOUN _____

PART OF THE BODY _____

PLURAL NOUN _____

NOUN _____

VERB _____

ADJECTIVE _____

NOUN _____

MAD LIBS®
WHY I BECAME A MONSTER,
BY LUMPY SPACE PRINCESS

Did I ever tell you about the time I became a/an _____-eating

NOUN

monster? It all started when my lumping _____ and I got into a

PLURAL NOUN

major _____ match. I was all, "_____ off!" and ran

VERB ENDING IN "ING"   VERB

away. Drama bomb! In (the) _____, some wolves took me under

A PLACE

their _____ . . . until they totally tried to _____ me

PLURAL NOUN   VERB

into shreds! Whatever, wolves. You never deserved my _____-

NOUN

ship! Finally I got away from those _____-stabbing wolves

PART OF THE BODY

and ended up in a field of fresh _____. The people there were all,

PLURAL NOUN

"Monster!" So I pretended I was one and ate everything but the kitchen

_____. Actually, I ate that, too. I was starving, okay? But

NOUN

being a monster was no _____ in the park. I was lonely and

VERB

_____. Everyone was so mad at me for stealing their food. So

ADJECTIVE

when my parents sent Jake and Finn to bring me home, I gave the people

some of the _____-wiches my parents packed with Finn. I'm so

NOUN

lumping nice sometimes, right?

From ADVENTURE TIME MAD LIBS® • ™ & © Cartoon Network. (s12). Published in 2012 by
Price Stern Sloan, an imprint of Penguin Random House LLC, 345 Hudson Street, New York, NY 10014.

MAD LIBS® is fun to play with friends, but you can also play it by yourself! To begin with, DO NOT look at the story on the page below. Fill in the blanks on this page with the words called for. Then, using the words you have selected, fill in the blank spaces in the story.

Now you've created your own hilarious MAD LIBS® game!

WHAT'S AWESOME ABOUT LADY RAINICORN, BY JAKE

NOUN _____

NOUN _____

VERB ENDING IN "ING" _____

ADJECTIVE _____

VERB _____

PART OF THE BODY _____

PLURAL NOUN _____

NOUN _____

NOUN _____

ADJECTIVE _____

ADJECTIVE _____

PLURAL NOUN _____

NOUN _____

NUMBER _____

ADJECTIVE _____

NOUN _____

ADJECTIVE _____

MAD LIBS®
WHAT'S AWESOME ABOUT
LADY RAINICORN, BY JAKE

Oh man. My _____-friend, Lady Rainicorn, is the coolest girl
          NOUN

I've ever met! She's a total babe and a smart _____, too. We love
                                                           NOUN

_____ viola duets together. It's kinda our thing. Her voice is so
VERB ENDING IN "ING"

soft and _____, I could _____ to it forever, y'know? I'd bend
           ADJECTIVE   VERB

over _____-ward for Lady. Cuz I'm stretchy and stuff. She helps
      PART OF THE BODY

_____ in trouble, too. Once Finn was being attacked by some
PLURAL NOUN

meanie Lake Knights, and she totally dove into the _____ and
                                                   NOUN

saved him! Did I mention how pretty she is? She's got _____-
                                                        NOUN

bow stripes on her body and a flowy, _____ mane. She smells
                                      ADJECTIVE

like _____ roses and straw. Plus, she flies, dude! And she can go
    ADJECTIVE

through _____ like a ghost!! And she can change any color with
       PLURAL NOUN

her magical _____!!! Yep, my lady is _____ of a kind.
          NOUN   NUMBER

I'm her _____ potato and she's my honey _____.
        ADJECTIVE   NOUN

We're mega-_____-hearts like that.
          ADJECTIVE

From ADVENTURE TIME MAD LIBS® • ™ & © Cartoon Network. (s12). Published in 2012 by
Price Stern Sloan, an imprint of Penguin Random House LLC, 345 Hudson Street, New York, NY 10014.

MAD LIBS® is fun to play with friends, but you can also play it by yourself! To begin with, DO NOT look at the story on the page below. Fill in the blanks on this page with the words called for. Then, using the words you have selected, fill in the blank spaces in the story.

Now you've created your own hilarious MAD LIBS® game!

BMO'S PRIMO FEATURES, BY BMO

VERB ENDING IN "ING" _____

PLURAL NOUN _____

ADJECTIVE _____

ADJECTIVE _____

NOUN _____

NOUN _____

NOUN _____

PLURAL NOUN _____

PART OF THE BODY (PLURAL) _____

PLURAL NOUN _____

NOUN _____

PLURAL NOUN _____

ADJECTIVE _____

PLURAL NOUN _____

ADJECTIVE _____

MAD LIBS®
BMO'S PRIMO FEATURES, BY BMO

Hi. I am BMO. I live with Jake and Finn. They spend hours

_____ video games on me. There are two _____
VERB ENDING IN "ING"   PLURAL NOUN

on my front for joysticks to plug into. Once, Jake and Finn made me

press my _____ button when they tickled me. This sent them
              ADJECTIVE

into a very _____ place—my main-brain-_____-
              ADJECTIVE   NOUN

frame! They went inside the video _____, but *whew!* they got
                                      NOUN

out alive. I am also alarm _____ for when it is time for Finn
                              NOUN

to take bath. I love to take pictures, too. The finished _____
                                                          PLURAL NOUN

shoot out of my _____. It is silly, but that is how I work!
                  PART OF THE BODY (PLURAL)

I can play VHS _____. We watched a whole lot of ones that the
                  PLURAL NOUN

_____ King made. He gives me heebie-_____. If you
      NOUN   PLURAL NOUN

need power source, I have extra _____ outlet! One thing I am
                                    ADJECTIVE

not is a place for Jake to rest his _____! I get _____
                                      PLURAL NOUN   ADJECTIVE

face when that happens. But mostly I am happy BMO and always have smile

for you!

MAD LIBS® is fun to play with friends, but you can also play it by yourself! To begin with, DO NOT look at the story on the page below. Fill in the blanks on this page with the words called for. Then, using the words you have selected, fill in the blank spaces in the story.

Now you've created your own hilarious MAD LIBS® game!

HOW TO WIN FRIENDS WITH LOTS OF TRYING AND A LITTLE MAGIC, BY ICE KING

VERB _____

NOUN _____

NOUN _____

NOUN _____

NOUN _____

ADJECTIVE _____

PLURAL NOUN _____

ADJECTIVE _____

NOUN _____

NOUN _____

NUMBER _____

VERB ENDING IN "ING" _____

NOUN _____

MAD LIBS®
HOW TO WIN FRIENDS
WITH LOTS OF TRYING AND
A LITTLE MAGIC, BY ICE KING

Wish you met someone who doesn't _____ in the other

VERB

direction when you arrive? Follow my solid-as-_____

NOUN

guidelines and watch your popularity _____-rocket!

NOUN

Rule #1: Every living _____ is a potential pal. If your only

NOUN

confidant is the reflection in your _____, try chatting up that

NOUN

_____ plant in the corner and see what happens! *Rule #2:* Don't

ADJECTIVE

be afraid to spy on _____ you'd like to know better. You'll learn

PLURAL NOUN

a lot about your _____ friend that way, and they'll be impressed

ADJECTIVE

you know what they ate for _____-fast! *Rule #3:* It's okay

NOUN

to ring someone's door-_____ more than _____

NOUN   NUMBER

times in a row even if you're not "invited." *Rule #4:* Nothing is wrong with

_____ your future friends with a freezing potion to make

VERB ENDING IN "ING"

'em stick around! *Rule #5:* Beg somebody, anybody, to throw you a/an

_____-day party. Don't stop until they do. It'll be the best party

NOUN

ever!

From ADVENTURE TIME MAD LIBS® • ™ & © Cartoon Network. (s12). Published in 2012 by
Price Stern Sloan, an imprint of Penguin Random House LLC, 345 Hudson Street, New York, NY 10014.

MAD LIBS® is fun to play with friends, but you can also play it by yourself! To begin with, DO NOT look at the story on the page below. Fill in the blanks on this page with the words called for. Then, using the words you have selected, fill in the blank spaces in the story.

Now you've created your own hilarious MAD LIBS® game!

WELCOME TO CANDY KINGDOM!

PLURAL NOUN _____

NOUN _____

VERB _____

NOUN _____

ADJECTIVE _____

PLURAL NOUN _____

NOUN _____

ADJECTIVE _____

NOUN _____

NOUN _____

ADJECTIVE _____

NOUN _____

ANIMAL _____

VERB ENDING IN "ING" _____

NOUN _____

ADJECTIVE _____

VERB ENDING IN "ING" _____

NOUN _____

MAD LIBS
WELCOME TO
CANDY KINGDOM!

Come meet the most sugary _____ in all of Ooo! Princess
                          PLURAL NOUN

Bubble-_____ is the leader of the Candy People. She is
        NOUN

kind and smart, but don't _____ her path! PB fights tooth and
                          VERB

_____ to shield her citizens from danger. The Banana Guards
NOUN

make sure no _____ guys get into the castle. They have
             ADJECTIVE

popsicle _____ for feet. Peppermint Butler is PB's personal
         PLURAL NOUN

_____. He has a/an _____ IQ and a mysterious past. Starchy
NOUN   ADJECTIVE

is a chocolate malt _____ and works in the cemetery as a/an
                    NOUN

_____-digger. Cinnamon Bun is a bit _____-baked
NOUN   ADJECTIVE

and isn't the smartest _____ in the shed. Science is a candy corn
                       NOUN

lab _____. He's really good at _____ formulas.
    ANIMAL   VERB ENDING IN "ING"

Mr. Cupcake is a/an _____-builder and likes to show off his large,
                    NOUN

_____ muscles. _____ under the weather? Nurse
ADJECTIVE   VERB ENDING IN "ING"

_____-cake, Dr. Ice Cream, and Dr. Princess keep everyone in tip-
NOUN

top shape!

From ADVENTURE TIME MAD LIBS® • ™ & © Cartoon Network. (s12). Published in 2012 by
Price Stern Sloan, an imprint of Penguin Random House LLC, 345 Hudson Street, New York, NY 10014.

MAD LIBS® is fun to play with friends, but you can also play it by yourself! To begin with, DO NOT look at the story on the page below. Fill in the blanks on this page with the words called for. Then, using the words you have selected, fill in the blank spaces in the story.

Now you've created your own hilarious MAD LIBS® game!

JAKE'S SWEETEST, STRETCHIEST MOVES

NOUN _____

ADJECTIVE _____

VERB ENDING IN "ING" _____

NOUN _____

NOUN _____

NUMBER _____

VERB _____

NOUN _____

VERB _____

NOUN _____

EXCLAMATION _____

ADVERB _____

NOUN _____

VERB _____

MAD LIBS®
JAKE'S SWEETEST, STRETCHIEST MOVES

Jake's not your average, run-of-the-_____ bulldog. Nope, he's got
                                        NOUN

_____ Powers! He was probably born with them, but Jake thinks
ADJECTIVE

he got them from _____ in a magic mud puddle. The powers
                  VERB ENDING IN "ING"

let Jake shape-shift into all sorts of things. If he needs to hide, he can

shrink himself down to fit inside Finn's front shirt _____. Or if
                                                     NOUN

Finn is in a sticky _____, Jake can inflate over _____
                    NOUN   NUMBER

times his regular size and help him out. Sometimes Jake's powers don't

_____ that well. To unlock a door, Jake can turn his hand into the
VERB

shape of a/an _____ . . . but it usually doesn't fit. Once, Jake and
              NOUN

Finn were stuck in BMO's video game and needed to _____ a pit.
                                                  VERB

Jake was able to stretch his _____ to safety. _____, right?
                             NOUN   EXCLAMATION

Then there was the time Jake stretched himself too _____ while in
                                                   ADVERB

a maze and almost kicked the _____. Mostly, he uses his powers to
                             NOUN

make Finn _____ really hard!
          VERB

From ADVENTURE TIME MAD LIBS® • ™ & © Cartoon Network. (s12). Published in 2012 by
Price Stern Sloan, an imprint of Penguin Random House LLC, 345 Hudson Street, New York, NY 10014.

MAD LIBS® is fun to play with friends, but you can also play it by yourself! To begin with, DO NOT look at the story on the page below. Fill in the blanks on this page with the words called for. Then, using the words you have selected, fill in the blank spaces in the story.

Now you've created your own hilarious MAD LIBS® game!

THE DAY WE ROCKED SO FLIPPIN' HARD, BY FINN

COLOR _____

PLURAL NOUN _____

NOUN _____

ADJECTIVE _____

ADJECTIVE _____

VERB _____

ADJECTIVE _____

VERB _____

VERB ENDING IN "ING" _____

PLURAL NOUN _____

PART OF THE BODY _____

ADJECTIVE _____

PLURAL NOUN _____

Ever hear about the time me and my buds formed a/an _____-

__COLOR__

hot band? It all started when a Door Lord stole our precious

_____. He took BMO's controller, Jake's baby _____,

__PLURAL NOUN__   __NOUN__

and, um, uh . . . a wad of Princess Bubblegum's _____ hair that

__ADJECTIVE__

I sometimes cuddle with. We stayed _____ on his trail. He

__ADJECTIVE__

lived behind a sealed door that said *"This door shall _____ to*

__VERB__

no command, save for a song from a/an _____ band." We had to

__ADJECTIVE__

_____ music together to bust open that door! First, everyone

__VERB__

was _____ like cats and _____. Then we realized

__VERB ENDING IN "ING"__   __PLURAL NOUN__

that not just any song would work—it had to be one that came from the

_____. So I started crooning about how everyone there was my

__PART OF THE BODY__

best friend in the whole, _____ world. My pals joined in, and

__ADJECTIVE__

the door opened! I think we all learned that the real treasure is being good

_____ together. But I'm glad I got PB's hair back.

__PLURAL NOUN__

MAD LIBS® is fun to play with friends, but you can also play it by yourself! To begin with, DO NOT look at the story on the page below. Fill in the blanks on this page with the words called for. Then, using the words you have selected, fill in the blank spaces in the story.

Now you've created your own hilarious MAD LIBS® game!

HOW TO PICK THE BEST HENCHMAN, BY MARCELINE

NOUN _____

ADJECTIVE _____

NOUN _____

NOUN _____

NUMBER _____

VERB _____

PLURAL NOUN _____

VERB _____

ADJECTIVE _____

PLURAL NOUN _____

PART OF THE BODY _____

NOUN _____

ADJECTIVE _____

NOUN _____

ADJECTIVE _____

PART OF THE BODY _____

NOUN _____

MAD LIBS®
HOW TO PICK THE BEST
HENCHMAN, BY MARCELINE

Need a side-_____ to do all your _____ work?
          NOUN   ADJECTIVE

Check out my tips on how to choose the right guy or _____ for
                                                        NOUN

the job.

1. Find someone who will go the extra _____ for you.
                                          NOUN

   It's good if they think you're _____ percent evil and you
                                        NUMBER

   _____ the living day-_____ out of them.
       VERB   PLURAL NOUN

2. If your henchman refuses to follow orders, _____ the
                                                    VERB

   command in a stern, _____ tone. It helps them listen better.
                          ADJECTIVE

3. The ideal henchman doesn't ask too many _____ or really use
                                               PLURAL NOUN

   their _____ to think at all.
          PART OF THE BODY

Finn was my best _____-man at first, but it didn't last because he
                    NOUN

got real _____ to my tricks! Having a henchman who is as sharp
            ADJECTIVE

as a/an _____ just doesn't last in the _____ run. Cuz
            NOUN   ADJECTIVE

once they realize that you're just pulling their _____ with the
                                                   PART OF THE BODY

whole "I'm a/an _____-sucking vampire" thing, your game is so up.
                    NOUN

From ADVENTURE TIME MAD LIBS® • ™ & © Cartoon Network. (s12). Published in 2012 by
Price Stern Sloan, an imprint of Penguin Random House LLC, 345 Hudson Street, New York, NY 10014.

MAD LIBS® is fun to play with friends, but you can also play it by yourself! To begin with, DO NOT look at the story on the page below. Fill in the blanks on this page with the words called for. Then, using the words you have selected, fill in the blank spaces in the story.

Now you've created your own hilarious MAD LIBS® game!

THE PERFECT PRANK, BY PRINCESS BUBBLEGUM

NUMBER _____

PART OF THE BODY _____

NOUN _____

ADJECTIVE _____

NOUN _____

ADJECTIVE _____

PLURAL NOUN _____

ADJECTIVE _____

VERB (PAST TENSE) _____

ADJECTIVE _____

NOUN _____

PLURAL NOUN _____

NUMBER _____

PLURAL NOUN _____

PART OF THE BODY _____

NOUN _____

MAD LIBS®
THE PERFECT PRANK,
BY PRINCESS BUBBLEGUM

When I aged myself down to _____ years old, things got a little

NUMBER

out of _____ in Candy Kingdom. The Earl of Lemongrab rode

PART OF THE BODY

in on his royal _____ and said I was too _____

NOUN ADJECTIVE

to rule! According to the rule _____, he was right. But the

NOUN

earl was a mean, _____ tyrant. I had to get him to pack up

ADJECTIVE

his _____ and leave for good. Finn and I decided to play

PLURAL NOUN

_____ pranks on him! First, we set up a machine where a boot

ADJECTIVE

_____ a marble, which set off a/an _____ reaction

VERB (PAST TENSE) ADJECTIVE

of motion. The final result was a note that sprang up for the earl to read.

It said "You smell like hot _____ buns." Then, we dressed up

NOUN

like spooky _____ and tried to scare him out of town. Well,

PLURAL NOUN

that didn't work! We were back to square _____. But we had one

NUMBER

more prank up our _____. We poured spicy serum right into his

PLURAL NOUN

_____. You could say he got a/an _____ of his own

PART OF THE BODY NOUN

medicine!

MAD LIBS® is fun to play with friends, but you can also play it by yourself! To begin with, DO NOT look at the story on the page below. Fill in the blanks on this page with the words called for. Then, using the words you have selected, fill in the blank spaces in the story.

Now you've created your own hilarious MAD LIBS® game!

ME VS. THE OCEAN, BY FINN

VERB (PAST TENSE) _____

PART OF THE BODY (PLURAL) _____

VERB _____

ADJECTIVE _____

NOUN _____

PLURAL NOUN _____

ADJECTIVE _____

EXCLAMATION _____

NOUN _____

VERB (PAST TENSE) _____

PART OF THE BODY _____

PART OF THE BODY _____

NOUN _____

ADJECTIVE _____

VERB ENDING IN "ING" _____

MAD LIBS®
ME VS. THE OCEAN, BY FINN

I didn't even know the ocean totally _____ me out until I
_____VERB (PAST TENSE)_____

tried to go in! When the waves came close, my _____
_____PART OF THE BODY (PLURAL)_____

trembled like crazy. So not math. How could I be a real hero if I didn't

_____ my fear? That's why I asked Jake for help. He took
VERB

me for a/an _____ submarine ride. We saw an abandoned
ADJECTIVE

old _____ and sea-_____. I was beginning
NOUN   PLURAL NOUN

to dig the ocean until Jake steered us into a deep, _____
ADJECTIVE

abyss! "_____!" I screamed. I pulled the emergency
EXCLAMATION

_____ on my diving suit and _____ to the surface.
NOUN   VERB (PAST TENSE)

All that commotion made Jake hit his _____ hard, knocking
PART OF THE BODY

him out! I had to save him, but my fear was huge. So I knocked myself

on the _____ with a/an _____ and landed near
PART OF THE BODY   NOUN

Jake. Once I realized where I was, I panicked. Jake pulled his cord, and

soon we were back on _____ land. Does being scared make
ADJECTIVE

me less than a hero? No _____ way!
VERB ENDING IN "ING"

MAD LIBS® is fun to play with friends, but you can also play it by yourself! To begin with, DO NOT look at the story on the page below. Fill in the blanks on this page with the words called for. Then, using the words you have selected, fill in the blank spaces in the story.

Now you've created your own hilarious MAD LIBS® game!

THE BLAME GAME, BY JAKE & FINN

COLOR _____

VERB (PAST TENSE) _____

PLURAL NOUN _____

PART OF THE BODY (PLURAL) _____

NOUN _____

VERB _____

ADJECTIVE _____

PLURAL NOUN _____

NOUN _____

ADJECTIVE _____

NOUN _____

VERB _____

MAD LIBS®
THE BLAME GAME,
BY JAKE & FINN

Finn: Yo, Jake, remember that time one of our righteous spells turned

Princess Bubblegum's skin _____ and her hair _____
                 COLOR   VERB (PAST TENSE)

out?

Jake: Oh yeah! And she blamed the Duke of _____ for it. Man,
                                            PLURAL NOUN

she hated his _____.
              PART OF THE BODY (PLURAL)

Finn: When she was all, "I won't forgive the _____ who did
                                       NOUN

this to me," I couldn't _____ up to the truth. We went after the
                          VERB

duke. Not my most _____ moment as a hero.
                    ADJECTIVE

Jake: S'ok. Even awesome _____ like us make mistakes.
                      PLURAL NOUN

Finn: We went to find the duke, and he was sweeter than _____!
                                         NOUN

Jake: Well, he did fess up to stealing all of PB's _____ pudding
                               ADJECTIVE

supply.

Finn: And we fessed up to PB for making her look like an ugly

_____.
      NOUN

Jake: And she didn't _____ it against us! But she still doesn't like the
                       VERB

duke. Whatevs!

From ADVENTURE TIME MAD LIBS® • ™ & © Cartoon Network. (s12). Published in 2012 by
Price Stern Sloan, an imprint of Penguin Random House LLC, 345 Hudson Street, New York, NY 10014.

MAD LIBS® is fun to play with friends, but you can also play it by yourself! To begin with, DO NOT look at the story on the page below. Fill in the blanks on this page with the words called for. Then, using the words you have selected, fill in the blank spaces in the story.

Now you've created your own hilarious MAD LIBS® game!

POEM FOR PRINCESS BUBBLEGUM, BY FINN

NOUN _____

ADJECTIVE _____

VERB _____

ADJECTIVE _____

PLURAL NOUN _____

VERB _____

NOUN _____

PART OF THE BODY (PLURAL) _____

VERB _____

PLURAL NOUN _____

ADJECTIVE _____

ADJECTIVE _____

NOUN _____

ADJECTIVE _____

Oh, PB, I miss the _____ we shared when you were thirteen.
NOUN

Your lips tasted so _____. Do you think we'll ever repeat that
ADJECTIVE

scene? There's so much to like about you, I can't even _____
VERB

that high. If I got on your _____ side, I think I'd just about
ADJECTIVE

die. Love that you love science. You're so math. Plus you fight the bad

_____ and all evil wrath. Whenever we _____ time
PLURAL NOUN   VERB

together, my heart goes *tick-tock-tick*. By now you gotta know that I think

you're so algebraic. Do you think it's weird that I have a/an _____
NOUN

of your hair? Or that when I look into your _____
PART OF THE BODY (PLURAL)

all I can do is _____ and stare? You can brush me off as a
VERB

crush, but my _____ won't disappear. No one can match your
PLURAL NOUN

_____ smile. Am I making myself clear? Basically you're the most
ADJECTIVE

_____ girl I've ever known. And if you don't like me more than
ADJECTIVE

a/an _____, I guess I'll just be alone. This poem you'll never see,
NOUN

it's way too _____ to share. Just know, that I'll always supercare.
ADJECTIVE

MAD LIBS® is fun to play with friends, but you can also play it by yourself! To begin with, DO NOT look at the story on the page below. Fill in the blanks on this page with the words called for. Then, using the words you have selected, fill in the blank spaces in the story.

Now you've created your own hilarious MAD LIBS® game!

THAT LUMPING BRAD!, BY LUMPY SPACE PRINCESS

NOUN _____

VERB ENDING IN "ING" _____

ADJECTIVE _____

NOUN _____

ADJECTIVE _____

NOUN _____

FIRST NAME (FEMALE) _____

VERB _____

NOUN _____

PART OF THE BODY (PLURAL) _____

ADJECTIVE _____

NOUN _____

NOUN _____

ADJECTIVE _____

PART OF THE BODY (PLURAL) _____

NOUN _____

MAD LIBS®
THAT LUMPING BRAD!,
BY LUMPY SPACE PRINCESS

What the _____, you guys! I can't stop _____
NOUN   _VERB ENDING IN "ING"_

about my stupid, _____ ex-boyfriend, Brad. He's like
                   ADJECTIVE

my best dream and my worst _____-mare all rolled up into
                           NOUN

one smallish, _____ body. I'm telling you, we were a/an
              ADJECTIVE

_____ made in space heaven! So why is he going out with
NOUN

my best friend, _____? I mean, I _____ her to
                FIRST NAME (FEMALE)   _VERB_

death, but she doesn't deserve him! Life is so unfair! She's always teasing

me about how she's Brad's girl-_____. It makes me cry my
                                NOUN

_____ out all the lumping time. And then my face gets
PART OF THE BODY (PLURAL)

all red and _____. I can't take it! They're probably eating chili
            ADJECTIVE

_____ fries like we used to do right now. Traitors! Can I tell
NOUN

you something? I broke up with Brad. But he broke my _____
                                                      NOUN

into a million teensy, _____ pieces! He kissed me on the
                       ADJECTIVE

_____, and I just wasn't ready. Oh my _____, you
PART OF THE BODY (PLURAL)   _NOUN_

guys, I want him back so bad!!

From ADVENTURE TIME MAD LIBS® • ™ & © Cartoon Network. (s12). Published in 2012 by
Price Stern Sloan, an imprint of Penguin Random House LLC, 345 Hudson Street, New York, NY 10014.

MAD LIBS® is fun to play with friends, but you can also play it by yourself! To begin with, DO NOT look at the story on the page below. Fill in the blanks on this page with the words called for. Then, using the words you have selected, fill in the blank spaces in the story.

Now you've created your own hilarious MAD LIBS® game!

COME HANG IN THE TREE FORT!

ADJECTIVE _____

PLURAL NOUN _____

NOUN _____

ADJECTIVE _____

COLOR _____

NOUN _____

VERB ENDING IN "ING" _____

NOUN _____

VERB _____

NOUN _____

NOUN _____

ADJECTIVE _____

VERB _____

NOUN _____

ADJECTIVE _____

NOUN _____

VERB _____

MAD LIBS®
COME HANG IN
THE TREE FORT!

Finn and Jake's tree fort is their home _____ home. The tree

                  ADJECTIVE

has lots of nooks and _____ to explore, so let's take a peek! The

           PLURAL NOUN

entrance is at the base of the _____ trunk. Once you're inside,

               NOUN

there are all sorts of treasures, like piles of _____ coins, old black-

                                ADJECTIVE

and-_____ TVs, and a uni-_____. A ladder leads

       COLOR   NOUN

up to the _____ room. That's where Finn and Jake have their

       VERB ENDING IN "ING"

weekly _____ club, play with BMO, and just generally hang.

        NOUN

In the kitchen, Jake likes to _____ up culinary masterpieces.

                   VERB

Climb another _____ to get to the bedroom. Finn snuggles up in

          NOUN

a sleeping _____, and Jake slumbers in a/an _____

        NOUN   ADJECTIVE

dresser drawer. Near the top of the tree, there's a/an _____-out boat

                                           VERB

with a tele-_____ to check out what's happening in the distance.

        NOUN

A few outdoor bridges provide _____ access to different floors. Of

                    ADJECTIVE

course, no fort would be complete without a roof for _____-gazing

                                        NOUN

and _____-butt dance parties!

     VERB

From ADVENTURE TIME MAD LIBS® • ™ & © Cartoon Network. (s12). Published in 2012 by
Price Stern Sloan, an imprint of Penguin Random House LLC, 345 Hudson Street, New York, NY 10014.

MAD LIBS® is fun to play with friends, but you can also play it by yourself! To begin with, DO NOT look at the story on the page below. Fill in the blanks on this page with the words called for. Then, using the words you have selected, fill in the blank spaces in the story.

Now you've created your own hilarious MAD LIBS® game!

HOW TO BE A HERO IN FIVE EASY STEPS

NOUN _____

VERB ENDING IN "ING" _____

VERB _____

NUMBER _____

ADJECTIVE _____

NOUN _____

NOUN _____

PLURAL NOUN _____

NOUN _____

ADJECTIVE _____

NOUN _____

NOUN _____

ADJECTIVE _____

VERB _____

NOUN _____

MAD LIBS®
HOW TO BE A HERO IN FIVE EASY STEPS

Go from a wrongteous zero to a happenin' _____ by

NOUN

_____ a few righteous rules!

VERB ENDING IN "ING"

1. No matter what, heroes will always _____ evil wherever it may

VERB

be. Even if evil is living _____ thousand miles away in a really

NUMBER

inconvenient location like the middle of a/an _____ desert or

ADJECTIVE

beneath a deep, smelly _____.

NOUN

2. Heroes don't have to put on a brave _____ all the time.

NOUN

But they still save the day even when they're feeling like giant scaredy

_____.

PLURAL NOUN

3. A hero puts his _____ on the line to protect anyone who needs

NOUN

help. Usually this includes little _____ ladies, a kidnapped

ADJECTIVE

_____, and your best friend.

NOUN

4. A hero makes someone feel like they're on top of the _____!

NOUN

5. It's okay for a hero to make a/an _____ mistake. Don't

ADJECTIVE

_____ yourself up if you mess up! Just get back on the right

VERB

_____ and soon you'll be all hero-y in no time! Shmowzow!

NOUN

The AMAZING WORLD OF GUMBALL
MAD LIBS®

PSS!
PRICE STERN SLOAN
An Imprint of Penguin Random House

MAD LIBS®

INSTRUCTIONS

MAD LIBS® is a game for people who don't like games!
It can be played by one, two, three, four, or forty.

• RIDICULOUSLY SIMPLE DIRECTIONS

In this tablet you will find stories containing blank spaces where words are left out. One player, the READER, selects one of these stories. The READER does not tell anyone what the story is about. Instead, he/she asks the other players, the WRITERS, to give him/her words. These words are used to fill in the blank spaces in the story.

• TO PLAY

The READER asks each WRITER in turn to call out a word—an adjective or a noun or whatever the space calls for—and uses them to fill in the blank spaces in the story. The result is a MAD LIBS® game.

When the READER then reads the completed MAD LIBS® game to the other players, they will discover that they have written a story that is fantastic, screamingly funny, shocking, silly, crazy, or just plain dumb—depending upon which words each WRITER called out.

• EXAMPLE (*Before* and *After*)

"_____!" he said _____
     EXCLAMATION   ADVERB

as he jumped into his convertible _____ and
                                      NOUN

drove off with his _____ wife.
                  ADJECTIVE

"_____OUCH_____!" he said _____STUPIDLY_____
     EXCLAMATION   ADVERB

as he jumped into his convertible _____CAT_____ and
                                      NOUN

drove off with his _____BRAVE_____ wife.
                  ADJECTIVE

QUICK REVIEW

In case you have forgotten what adjectives, adverbs, nouns, and verbs are, here is a quick review:

An ADJECTIVE describes something or somebody. *Lumpy, soft, ugly, messy,* and *short* are adjectives.

An ADVERB tells how something is done. It modifies a verb and usually ends in "ly." *Modestly, stupidly, greedily,* and *carefully* are adverbs.

A NOUN is the name of a person, place, or thing. *Sidewalk, umbrella, bridle, bathtub,* and *nose* are nouns.

A VERB is an action word. *Run, pitch, jump,* and *swim* are verbs. Put the verbs in past tense if the directions say PAST TENSE. *Ran, pitched, jumped,* and *swam* are verbs in the past tense.

When we ask for A PLACE, we mean any sort of place: a country or city *(Spain, Cleveland)* or a room *(bathroom, kitchen).*

An EXCLAMATION or SILLY WORD is any sort of funny sound, gasp, grunt, or outcry, like *Wow!, Ouch!, Whomp!, Ick!,* and *Gadzooks!*

When we ask for specific words, like a NUMBER, a COLOR, an ANIMAL, or a PART OF THE BODY, we mean a word that is one of those things, like *seven, blue, horse,* or *head.*

When we ask for a PLURAL, it means more than one. For example, *cat* pluralized is *cats.*

MAD LIBS® is fun to play with friends, but you can also play it by yourself! To begin with, DO NOT look at the story on the page below. Fill in the blanks on this page with the words called for. Then, using the words you have selected, fill in the blank spaces in the story.

Now you've created your own hilarious MAD LIBS® game!

MEET THE WATTERSONS

ADJECTIVE _____

SAME ADJECTIVE _____

VERB _____

PERSON IN ROOM (FEMALE) _____

COLOR _____

ANIMAL _____

PLURAL NOUN _____

NUMBER _____

COLOR _____

COLOR _____

ADJECTIVE _____

PLURAL NOUN _____

ADJECTIVE _____

PLURAL NOUN _____

VERB ENDING IN "ING" _____

VERB _____

PART OF THE BODY (PLURAL) _____

NOUN _____

MAD LIBS®
MEET THE WATTERSONS

The Wattersons are a totally _____ family—right? It depends on

ADJECTIVE

your definition of _____! Even though they _____ like

SAME ADJECTIVE   VERB

humans, they most definitely are not! Mom (_____) is

PERSON IN ROOM (FEMALE)

a/an _____ cat, and Dad (Richard) is a pink _____. They

COLOR   ANIMAL

have three _____: Gumball, who is a blue _____-year-old

PLURAL NOUN   NUMBER

cat; Darwin, a/an _____-fish; and Anais, a/an _____ rabbit.

COLOR   COLOR

The Wattersons live in a typical family home in a typical _____

ADJECTIVE

neighborhood. They face the same trials and _____ that every

PLURAL NOUN

family does, from _____family dinners and family _____

ADJECTIVE   PLURAL NOUN

out to _____ chores and watching TV together. They may

VERB ENDING IN "ING"

_____ now and then, but they love each other and always have each

VERB

others' _____. And those fights usually end in a big group

PART OF THE BODY (PLURAL)

_____!

NOUN

From THE AMAZING WORLD OF GUMBALL MAD LIBS® • ™ & © TBS Europe Ltd, Cartoon Network. (s14).
Published in 2014 by Price Stern Sloan, an imprint of Penguin Random House LLC, 345 Hudson Street, New York, NY 10014.

MAD LIBS® is fun to play with friends, but you can also play it by yourself! To begin with, DO NOT look at the story on the page below. Fill in the blanks on this page with the words called for. Then, using the words you have selected, fill in the blank spaces in the story.

Now you've created your own hilarious MAD LIBS® game!

DEAR MOM, LOVE, GUMBALL

NOUN _____

ADJECTIVE _____

PLURAL NOUN _____

ADJECTIVE _____

NOUN _____

ADJECTIVE _____

VERB _____

NOUN _____

VERB _____

ADVERB _____

ADJECTIVE _____

ADJECTIVE _____

PART OF THE BODY _____

ANIMAL _____

NOUN _____

MAD LIBS®
DEAR MOM,
LOVE, GUMBALL

Dear Mom,

I just wanted to write you a/an _____ to let you know that even
                                    NOUN

though I am not always an angel with a/an _____ halo and
                                            ADJECTIVE

_____, I try my very best to act _____ and be the best
PLURAL NOUN   ADJECTIVE

_____ possible. I know that I can be a/an _____ handful at
NOUN   ADJECTIVE

times because I _____ accidents, create trouble for the _____,
                  VERB   NOUN

have a tendency to _____ things, and often hurt myself (and everyone
                      VERB

else in the family!), but I _____ mean well. And because I'm a/an
                              ADVERB

_____ blue cat, just like you, I always try to make you _____
ADJECTIVE   ADJECTIVE

and follow in your _____-steps by being the very best blue _____
                     PART OF THE BODY   ANIMAL

I can be.

Love from your favorite _____,
                          NOUN

Gumball

MAD LIBS® is fun to play with friends, but you can also play it by yourself! To begin with, DO NOT look at the story on the page below. Fill in the blanks on this page with the words called for. Then, using the words you have selected, fill in the blank spaces in the story.

Now you've created your own hilarious MAD LIBS® game!

DEAR MOM, LOVE, DARWIN

VERB _____

PART OF THE BODY _____

SAME PART OF THE BODY _____

NOUN _____

VERB _____

ADJECTIVE _____

VERB ENDING IN "ING" _____

SAME VERB ENDING IN "ING" _____

ADJECTIVE _____

ADJECTIVE _____

PLURAL NOUN _____

VERB _____

NOUN _____

ADJECTIVE _____

MAD LIBS®
DEAR MOM,
LOVE, DARWIN

Dear Mom,

I just wanted to _____ you a letter to let you know that Gumball
                    VERB

twisted my _____ to get me to help him write his letter. (And he really
           PART OF THE BODY

did twist my _____.) He said that if I didn't help him, he
             SAME PART OF THE BODY

would make me clean our _____ and _____ all his chores for
                        NOUN   VERB

him. I feel a little _____ for _____ on him, because
                     ADJECTIVE   VERB ENDING IN "ING"

I don't like _____ on Gumball. After all, he's a/an
             SAME VERB ENDING IN "ING"

_____ brother. Even if he does put me in _____ situations,
ADJECTIVE   ADJECTIVE

include me in his crazy _____, and make me _____ for
                        PLURAL NOUN   VERB

him, he is still the best _____ ever.
                          NOUN

Love from your _____ son,
               ADJECTIVE

Darwin

MAD LIBS® is fun to play with friends, but you can also play it by yourself! To begin with, DO NOT look at the story on the page below. Fill in the blanks on this page with the words called for. Then, using the words you have selected, fill in the blank spaces in the story.

Now you've created your own hilarious MAD LIBS® game!

DON'T FORGET ANAIS

NUMBER _____

NOUN _____

ADVERB _____

NOUN _____

ADVERB _____

PLURAL NOUN _____

ADJECTIVE _____

NOUN _____

NOUN _____

NOUN _____

SAME NOUN _____

NOUN _____

ADJECTIVE _____

ADJECTIVE _____

VERB _____

ADJECTIVE _____

NOUN _____

VERB _____

MAD LIBS®
DON'T FORGET ANAIS

At only _____ years old, Anais may be the youngest
                    NUMBER

_____ of the Watterson family, but she is _____ the smartest.
    NOUN   ADVERB

In fact, she's kind of a/an _____! Anais _____ looks after
                               NOUN   ADVERB

her two _____ and her dad while her mom is at work every day.
          PLURAL NOUN

She has to help her _____ brothers with their _____-work
                      ADJECTIVE   NOUN

and make breakfast for her _____. She is in the junior kindergarten
                              NOUN

_____ at school, just down the hallway from Gumball's
    NOUN

_____, and she is a member of the _____ Club. Daisy, a
  SAME NOUN   NOUN

purple _____ toy donkey, is Anais's _____ companion. Don't
          ADJECTIVE   ADJECTIVE

ever _____ with Daisy, because Anais has a/an _____ temper
        VERB   ADJECTIVE

(which she gets from her _____!) and she will _____ you if
                            NOUN   VERB

she has to.

From THE AMAZING WORLD OF GUMBALL MAD LIBS® • ™ & © TBS Europe Ltd, Cartoon Network. (s14).
Published in 2014 by Price Stern Sloan, an imprint of Penguin Random House LLC, 345 Hudson Street, New York, NY 10014.

MAD LIBS® is fun to play with friends, but you can also play it by yourself! To begin with, DO NOT look at the story on the page below. Fill in the blanks on this page with the words called for. Then, using the words you have selected, fill in the blank spaces in the story.

Now you've created your own hilarious MAD LIBS® game!

GOOD OLE
RICHARD WATTERSON

PART OF THE BODY _____

SAME PART OF THE BODY _____

TYPE OF FOOD _____

SAME TYPE OF FOOD _____

PLURAL NOUN _____

PLURAL NOUN _____

NOUN _____

ADVERB _____

NOUN _____

VERB ENDING IN "ING" _____

ADJECTIVE _____

VERB _____

SILLY WORD _____

VERB ENDING IN "ING" _____

NOUN _____

VERB _____

MAD LIBS®
GOOD OLE
RICHARD WATTERSON

Survey Taker: I'd like to speak to the _____ of the household.
<u>PART OF THE BODY</u>

Richard: I have a/an _____.
<u>SAME PART OF THE BODY</u>

Survey Taker: Are you the _____-winner at this address?
<u>TYPE OF FOOD</u>

Richard: Well, I've never won any _____, but I'm really

good at *Space* _____.
<u>PLURAL NOUN</u>

Survey Taker: Sir, I'm hoping you might be able to answer some simple

_____ about how your family spends their _____.
<u>PLURAL NOUN</u>   <u>NOUN</u>

Richard: I _____ do nothing. Does that count?
<u>ADVERB</u>

Survey Taker: That isn't really the _____ I'm asking.
<u>NOUN</u>

Richard: I'm not very good at _____. I leave that to my
<u>VERB ENDING IN "ING"</u>

_____ wife, Nicole.
<u>ADJECTIVE</u>

Survey Taker: Is she there? Would I be able to _____ with her?
<u>VERB</u>

Richard: _____, I'm not sure. Let me check. *NICOLE!*
<u>SILLY WORD</u>

Anais: Dad, Mom is out _____, just like every day.
<u>VERB ENDING IN "ING"</u>

Richard: Oh yeah, my wife is the bread-_____ at this address.
<u>NOUN</u>

Survey Taker: I will _____ for her. Good-bye. [*Click.*]
<u>VERB</u>

FROM THE AMAZING WORLD OF GUMBALL MAD LIBS® • ™ & © TBS Europe Ltd, Cartoon Network. (s14).
Published in 2014 by Price Stern Sloan, an imprint of Penguin Random House LLC, 345 Hudson Street, New York, NY 10014.

MAD LIBS® is fun to play with friends, but you can also play it by yourself! To begin with, DO NOT look at the story on the page below. Fill in the blanks on this page with the words called for. Then, using the words you have selected, fill in the blank spaces in the story.

Now you've created your own hilarious MAD LIBS® game!

NICOLE WATTERSON

ADJECTIVE _____

VERB ENDING IN "ING" _____

ADJECTIVE _____

PLURAL NOUN _____

NOUN _____

VERB _____

PLURAL NOUN _____

ADJECTIVE _____

ADJECTIVE _____

NOUN _____

TYPE OF FOOD _____

PLURAL NOUN _____

PLURAL NOUN _____

ADJECTIVE _____

ANIMAL _____

PART OF THE BODY (PLURAL) _____

MAD LIBS
NICOLE WATTERSON

The Wattersons are a very _____ family to have Nicole
                              ADJECTIVE
_____ after them. She is smart and _____, and she
  VERB ENDING IN "ING"   ADJECTIVE

will do whatever it takes to look after her _____. Nicole does have
                                              PLURAL NOUN

a bit of a/an _____, and she has been known to _____ off
                NOUN   VERB

the handle sometimes. But no matter what, she always forgives her two

troublemaking _____ and slightly _____ husband. Nicole
                PLURAL NOUN   ADJECTIVE

Watterson works _____ hours at the Rainbow Factory as a sales-
                    ADJECTIVE

_____ to bring home the _____ for her family. She will
    NOUN   TYPE OF FOOD

defend her _____ to the death. She even stood up to Miss Simian,
              PLURAL NOUN

who called the Wattersons a bunch of _____! And even though she
                                        PLURAL NOUN

is very _____, Nicole never learned to ride a/an _____. She
          ADJECTIVE   ANIMAL

just sits on it and runs with her own _____!
                                         PART OF THE BODY (PLURAL)

MAD LIBS® is fun to play with friends, but you can also play it by yourself! To begin with, DO NOT look at the story on the page below. Fill in the blanks on this page with the words called for. Then, using the words you have selected, fill in the blank spaces in the story.

Now you've created your own hilarious MAD LIBS® game!

I LOVE YOU, PENNY FITZGERALD, BY GUMBALL

PLURAL NOUN _____

NOUN _____

PART OF THE BODY _____

VERB _____

PART OF THE BODY _____

VERB _____

ADJECTIVE _____

NOUN _____

VERB _____

ADJECTIVE _____

NOUN _____

SAME NOUN _____

VERB _____

NOUN _____

NOUN _____

PERSON IN ROOM (MALE) _____

MAD LIBS®
I LOVE YOU, PENNY FITZGERALD, BY GUMBALL

Dear Penny,

My adorable little peanut with _____. You are the _____
                              PLURAL NOUN   NOUN

of my dreams, and you make my _____ skip a beat every time I
                              PART OF THE BODY

_____ you. Could you ever see it in your heart (do you have a/an
VERB

_____ ?) to _____ a/an _____ blue cat like me? You
PART OF THE BODY   VERB   ADJECTIVE

are the best cheer-_____ , and when I see you _____ your
                   NOUN   VERB

pom-poms, it makes me go all _____ . I'm sorry that the _____
                             ADJECTIVE   NOUN

that was home to your _____-house girls' club got cut down—I would
                      SAME NOUN

_____ you another one if I could. I know that your _____
VERB   NOUN

doesn't really like me, but I'm hoping that someday I can win him over and get

him to see that you and I would be the best _____ ever.
                                            NOUN

Yours forever,

_____
PERSON IN ROOM (MALE)

MAD LIBS® is fun to play with friends, but you can also play it by yourself! To begin with, DO NOT look at the story on the page below. Fill in the blanks on this page with the words called for. Then, using the words you have selected, fill in the blank spaces in the story.

Now you've created your own hilarious MAD LIBS® game!

ELMORE JUNIOR HIGH

ADJECTIVE _____

PLURAL NOUN _____

NOUN _____

PART OF THE BODY _____

ADJECTIVE _____

PLURAL NOUN _____

PLURAL NOUN _____

NOUN _____

ADJECTIVE _____

PLURAL NOUN _____

PLURAL NOUN _____

ADJECTIVE _____

PERSON IN ROOM (FEMALE) _____

NOUN _____

NOUN _____

VERB ENDING IN "ING" _____

NOUN _____

PLURAL NOUN _____

MAD LIBS®
ELMORE JUNIOR HIGH

Elmore Junior High is the town of Elmore's _____ middle school.
ADJECTIVE

Gumball, Darwin, and Anais all go there, and so did their _____.
PLURAL NOUN

Darwin and Gumball are in Miss Simian's seventh-grade _____. She
NOUN

rules her classroom with an iron _____—and a very _____
PART OF THE BODY   ADJECTIVE

voice! Although Anais is only four _____ old, she also attends
PLURAL NOUN

Elmore and is in a junior kindergarten class down the hall from her

_____. Principal Brown is the _____ at Elmore Junior
PLURAL NOUN   NOUN

High. He is a slug with a/an _____ coat of brown _____,
ADJECTIVE   PLURAL NOUN

and he can't see without his thick, round _____. He has a/an
PLURAL NOUN

_____ crush on _____. Gross. Mr. Small is the
ADJECTIVE   PERSON IN ROOM (FEMALE)

school guidance _____, even though *he's* the one who needs the most
NOUN

guidance. And there's a club for every _____ at Elmore Junior High,
NOUN

like the Reject Club and the Synchronized _____ Club.
VERB ENDING IN "ING"

Elmore Junior High even has a school mascot, a/an _____. Go,
NOUN

_____!
PLURAL NOUN

MAD LIBS® is fun to play with friends, but you can also play it by yourself! To begin with, DO NOT look at the story on the page below. Fill in the blanks on this page with the words called for. Then, using the words you have selected, fill in the blank spaces in the story.

Now you've created your own hilarious MAD LIBS® game!

CLASSMATES

ADJECTIVE _____

PLURAL NOUN _____

PART OF THE BODY _____

ADJECTIVE _____

TYPE OF FOOD _____

NOUN _____

ADJECTIVE _____

NOUN _____

PERSON IN ROOM (FEMALE) _____

ADJECTIVE _____

PART OF THE BODY (PLURAL) _____

PLURAL NOUN _____

NOUN _____

PART OF THE BODY _____

ADJECTIVE _____

NOUN _____

ADJECTIVE _____

MAD LIBS®
CLASSMATES

Meet Gumball and Darwin's classmates at Elmore Junior High:

- Penny—Gumball's crush, who is a/an _____ peanut with a set of
  ADJECTIVE
  _____ growing out of her _____
  PLURAL NOUN   PART OF THE BODY

- Anton—a/an _____ piece of _____
  ADJECTIVE   TYPE OF FOOD

- Tina—the school _____, and a/an _____ T. rex
  NOUN   ADJECTIVE

- Banana Joe—the class _____, who loves playing jokes
  NOUN

- Tobias—the class jock, who also has a crush on _____
  PERSON IN ROOM (FEMALE)

- Alan—a/an _____ balloon, whose lack of _____
  ADJECTIVE   PART OF THE BODY (PLURAL)
  often causes him problems

- Carmen—the leader of the _____ at school
  PLURAL NOUN

- Bobert—the smartest _____ in the class
  NOUN

- William—a mysterious flying _____, who likes to spy on his
  PART OF THE BODY
  classmates

- Ocho—a/an _____ but tough 8-_____ spider. He's a
  ADJECTIVE   NOUN
  good guy as long as you stay on his _____ side.
  ADJECTIVE

From THE AMAZING WORLD OF GUMBALL MAD LIBS® • ™ & © TBS Europe Ltd, Cartoon Network. (s14).
Published in 2014 by Price Stern Sloan, an imprint of Penguin Random House LLC, 345 Hudson Street, New York, NY 10014.

MAD LIBS® is fun to play with friends, but you can also play it by yourself! To begin with, DO NOT look at the story on the page below. Fill in the blanks on this page with the words called for. Then, using the words you have selected, fill in the blank spaces in the story.

Now you've created your own hilarious MAD LIBS® game!

MY HISTORY ESSAY, BY GUMBALL

ADJECTIVE _____

NOUN _____

PERSON IN ROOM (MALE) _____

ARTICLE OF CLOTHING (PLURAL) _____

PLURAL NOUN _____

SAME PLURAL NOUN _____

PERSON IN ROOM (MALE) _____

PERSON IN ROOM (MALE) _____

NOUN _____

PERSON IN ROOM (FEMALE) _____

NOUN _____

PLURAL NOUN _____

NOUN _____

NOUN _____

ADJECTIVE _____

PLURAL NOUN _____

MAD LIBS
MY HISTORY ESSAY, BY GUMBALL

The American Revolution was a/an _____ event in the history of our
_____ADJECTIVE_____

_____. It started when _____ Washington decided he
NOUN   PERSON IN ROOM (MALE)

didn't like the British and their red _____ anymore. And
ARTICLE OF CLOTHING (PLURAL)

Mr. Washington also didn't like paying _____ to the British—my
PLURAL NOUN

dad doesn't like paying _____, either. Washington asked his
SAME PLURAL NOUN

friends _____ Jefferson and _____ Franklin to
PERSON IN ROOM (MALE)   PERSON IN ROOM (MALE)

help him write a/an _____ of Independence, and he asked a woman
NOUN

named _____ Ross to sew him a/an _____. It was a
PERSON IN ROOM (FEMALE)   NOUN

good thing she liked _____ and stripes, otherwise we might have
PLURAL NOUN

had a/an _____ with polka dots and flowers. Luckily, Mr. Washington
NOUN

won the American _____, because otherwise we would all have
NOUN

_____ accents and be forced to eat overcooked _____ all
ADJECTIVE   PLURAL NOUN

the time.

From THE AMAZING WORLD OF GUMBALL MAD LIBS® • ™ & © TBS Europe Ltd, Cartoon Network. (s14).
Published in 2014 by Price Stern Sloan, an imprint of Penguin Random House LLC, 345 Hudson Street, New York, NY 10014.

MAD LIBS® is fun to play with friends, but you can also play it by yourself! To begin with, DO NOT look at the story on the page below. Fill in the blanks on this page with the words called for. Then, using the words you have selected, fill in the blank spaces in the story.

Now you've created your own hilarious MAD LIBS® game!

KARATE WIENERS

ADJECTIVE _____

PLURAL NOUN _____

VERB ENDING IN "ING" _____

ADJECTIVE _____

PLURAL NOUN _____

ADJECTIVE _____

VERB ENDING IN "ING" _____

NUMBER _____

VERB _____

PLURAL NOUN _____

PLURAL NOUN _____

ANIMAL (PLURAL) _____

A PLACE _____

ADJECTIVE _____

MAD LIBS®
KARATE WIENERS

Gumball: Remember that time we asked Mom to buy us super _____

ADJECTIVE

karate _____?

PLURAL NOUN

Darwin: Yeah, she was worried that we'd get bored with it, like we did with

football, tennis, and figure-_____.

VERB ENDING IN "ING"

Gumball: But we looked totally _____ in our outfits. Girls totally dig

ADJECTIVE

guys with karate _____.

PLURAL NOUN

Darwin: Yeah, we had some _____ moves.

ADJECTIVE

Gumball: Mom was worried that we would waste our lives and still be

_____ at home in _____ years.

VERB ENDING IN "ING"   NUMBER

Darwin: Yeah, it was hard to _____ our martial arts _____

VERB   PLURAL NOUN

good-bye.

Gumball: But we weren't really that good, and everyone at school called us tae

kwon _____.

PLURAL NOUN

Darwin: Hey, maybe we could ask Mom about buying us some polo

_____. We could keep them in (the) _____.

ANIMAL (PLURAL)   A PLACE

Gumball: That's a/an _____ idea, bro.

ADJECTIVE

MAD LIBS® is fun to play with friends, but you can also play it by yourself! To begin with, DO NOT look at the story on the page below. Fill in the blanks on this page with the words called for. Then, using the words you have selected, fill in the blank spaces in the story.

Now you've created your own hilarious MAD LIBS® game!

CONTROL OF THE REMOTE CONTROL

PLURAL NOUN _____

ADJECTIVE _____

NOUN _____

VERB _____

SAME VERB _____

SILLY WORD _____

ADJECTIVE _____

PART OF THE BODY _____

NOUN _____

VERB ENDING IN "ING" _____

NOUN _____

PERSON IN ROOM (MALE) _____

PERSON IN ROOM (FEMALE) _____

ADJECTIVE _____

NOUN _____

NOUN _____

The Wattersons are devoted TV _____.
 PLURAL NOUN
Gumball and Darwin are fans of _____ *Pets*, Anais won't miss an episode of *Daisy the*
 ADJECTIVE
_____, Nicole loves _____ *or Don't* _____, and
 NOUN   _VERB_   _SAME VERB_
Richard is devoted to *La Casa de las* _____. Although Richard may
 SILLY WORD
not be very _____, when it comes to parking his _____ on
 ADJECTIVE   _PART OF THE BODY_
the family _____ and _____ the remote control, he is
 NOUN   _VERB ENDING IN "ING"_
tough to beat. Especially when he hides the remote in Butt _____.
 NOUN
But there is one member of the family who can outsmart _____
 PERSON IN ROOM (MALE)
when it comes to the remote: _____. That _____
 PERSON IN ROOM (FEMALE)   _ADJECTIVE_
girl tricked her family into thinking a garage-_____ opener was the
 NOUN
remote. So it looks like everyone will have to watch *Daisy the* _____
 NOUN
tonight . . .

From THE AMAZING WORLD OF GUMBALL MAD LIBS® • ™ & © TBS Europe Ltd, Cartoon Network. (s14).
Published in 2014 by Price Stern Sloan, an imprint of Penguin Random House LLC, 345 Hudson Street, New York, NY 10014.

MAD LIBS® is fun to play with friends, but you can also play it by yourself! To begin with, DO NOT look at the story on the page below. Fill in the blanks on this page with the words called for. Then, using the words you have selected, fill in the blank spaces in the story.

Now you've created your own hilarious MAD LIBS® game!

FUN, FUN, FUN!

ADJECTIVE _____

PLURAL NOUN _____

PLURAL NOUN _____

VERB _____

ADJECTIVE _____

NOUN _____

SAME NOUN _____

PART OF THE BODY (PLURAL) _____

EXCLAMATION _____

TYPE OF FOOD _____

PART OF THE BODY _____

ADJECTIVE _____

NOUN _____

TYPE OF FOOD _____

VERB _____

SAME VERB _____

VERB ENDING IN "ING" _____

NOUN _____

The Wattersons are a family who love _____ old-fashioned fun,
                                         ADJECTIVE

whether it's watching game shows, playing video _____, or rolling
                                                   PLURAL NOUN

the _____ for a board game. One of Gumball and Darwin's favorite
      PLURAL NOUN

games is _____ or Dare. It's a/an _____ game without any
           VERB   ADJECTIVE

official rules. A player rolls the dice, then picks a/an _____ from the
                                                          NOUN

stack. If the player chooses not to do what the _____ says, another
                                                  SAME NOUN

player must convince them to do something else, like catch a ball without

using their _____. _____! And then there's
              PART OF THE BODY (PLURAL)   EXCLAMATION

_____ *Fighter*, one of the Wattersons' favorite video games. It's a/an
TYPE OF FOOD

_____-off between a/an _____ rat that looks like a/an
PART OF THE BODY   ADJECTIVE

_____ and a/an _____ with eyes and mustard hair. And don't
NOUN   TYPE OF FOOD

forget the TV show _____ *or Don't* _____ hosted by the
                     VERB   SAME VERB

_____ Star. It was a/an _____ come true for Richard
VERB ENDING IN "ING"   NOUN

to appear on the show, even if he was a loser.

MAD LIBS® is fun to play with friends, but you can also play it by yourself! To begin with, DO NOT look at the story on the page below. Fill in the blanks on this page with the words called for. Then, using the words you have selected, fill in the blank spaces in the story.

Now you've created your own hilarious MAD LIBS® game!

MEET THE NEIGHBORS

ADJECTIVE _____

NOUN _____

ADJECTIVE _____

PERSON IN ROOM (MALE) _____

NOUN _____

PERSON IN ROOM (FEMALE) _____

PLURAL NOUN _____

NOUN _____

VERB ENDING IN "ING" _____

NOUN _____

PLURAL NOUN _____

VERB _____

MAD LIBS®
MEET THE NEIGHBORS

Mr. Robinson: I tell you, the neighborhood hasn't been the same since those

_____ Wattersons moved in.
<u>ADJECTIVE</u>

Mrs. Robinson: You're so right, my _____. They're loud, messy, and
<u>NOUN</u>

_____.
<u>ADJECTIVE</u>

Mr. Robinson: That _____ Watterson. He's a total waste of
<u>PERSON IN ROOM (MALE)</u>

_____.
<u>NOUN</u>

Mrs. Robinson: Yes, I feel badly for that wife of his, _____.
<u>PERSON IN ROOM (FEMALE)</u>

She does everything for him!

Mr. Robinson: And those _____ are nothing but trouble. They're
<u>PLURAL NOUN</u>

always throwing their toys into our _____.
<u>NOUN</u>

Mrs. Robinson: Not to mention they're always _____ into
<u>VERB ENDING IN "ING"</u>

our expensive, brand-new _____.
<u>NOUN</u>

Mr. Robinson: If they do that again, I'm going to have to call the

_____.
<u>PLURAL NOUN</u>

Rocky Robinson: Hey, Mom and Dad, can I go next door and _____
<u>VERB</u>

with Gumball and Darwin?

Published in 2014 by Price Stern Sloan, an imprint of Penguin Random House LLC, 345 Hudson Street, New York, NY 10014.

MAD LIBS® is fun to play with friends, but you can also play it by yourself! To begin with, DO NOT look at the story on the page below. Fill in the blanks on this page with the words called for. Then, using the words you have selected, fill in the blank spaces in the story.

Now you've created your own hilarious MAD LIBS® game!

FACING THE CONSEQUENCES, BY DARWIN

PLURAL NOUN _____

ADJECTIVE _____

VERB ENDING IN "ING" _____

PLURAL NOUN _____

PLURAL NOUN _____

NOUN _____

PERSON IN ROOM _____

NOUN _____

ADVERB _____

PLURAL NOUN _____

COLOR _____

ADJECTIVE _____

ADJECTIVE _____

VERB ENDING IN "ING" _____

ADJECTIVE _____

VERB _____

NOUN _____

MAD LIBS®
FACING THE CONSEQUENCES,
BY DARWIN

My brother, Gumball, has trouble understanding that he has to face the

consequences of his _____ . Gumball is _____ at
                PLURAL NOUN   ADJECTIVE

_____ mayhem, strategizing _____ , and
VERB ENDING IN "ING"   PLURAL NOUN

concocting _____ . That goes for everything from skipping out of
              PLURAL NOUN

_____ -work to getting _____ to do his home-_____ .
NOUN   PERSON IN ROOM   NOUN

But usually his plans go _____ wrong, and Gumball ends up in more
                            ADVERB

trouble than ever before! But rather than own up to his _____ , he
                                                 PLURAL NOUN

tells more _____ lies, which only makes everything _____ !
            COLOR   ADJECTIVE

Gumball has to learn that being _____ and _____
                           ADJECTIVE   VERB ENDING IN "ING"

the truth is a lot less _____ (and makes it easier to _____ at
                ADJECTIVE   VERB

night). What's that, Gumball? You want me to help you play a/an _____
                                                                  NOUN

on Dad? I'll be right there.

MAD LIBS® is fun to play with friends, but you can also play it by yourself! To begin with, DO NOT look at the story on the page below. Fill in the blanks on this page with the words called for. Then, using the words you have selected, fill in the blank spaces in the story.

Now you've created your own hilarious MAD LIBS® game!

SNACK TIME!

PLURAL NOUN _____

PLURAL NOUN _____

NOUN _____

ADJECTIVE _____

NOUN _____

ADJECTIVE _____

PERSON IN ROOM (MALE) _____

ADJECTIVE _____

ADJECTIVE _____

PERSON IN ROOM (MALE) _____

ADJECTIVE _____

NOUN _____

ADJECTIVE _____

NOUN _____

PERSON IN ROOM _____

MAD LIBS
SNACK TIME!

No matter what we're doing, we Wattersons sure like to eat. Some of our favorite

_____ are:
__PLURAL NOUN__

- Daisy _____—the perfect breakfast _____
  __PLURAL NOUN__   __NOUN__

- Pizza—_____ no matter what time of day!
  __ADJECTIVE__

- Chips—must be eaten straight out of the _____
  __NOUN__

- Lots and lots of _____ soda in every flavor!
  __ADJECTIVE__

- Doughnuts—beware, _____ will eat all of them if you're
  __PERSON IN ROOM (MALE)__

  not _____ enough
  __ADJECTIVE__

- Fish flakes (or _____ fish flakes)—only _____ eats
  __ADJECTIVE__   __PERSON IN ROOM (MALE)__

  those . . .

- School lunches—can actually be very _____, especially when you
  __ADJECTIVE__

  share them with your _____
  __NOUN__

- Anything from a trash can—it can be _____ when you've been
  __ADJECTIVE__

  lost in the Forest of _____
  __NOUN__

- Be careful of Jelly O' the Month made by _____—it can take
  __PERSON IN ROOM__

over the town!

From THE AMAZING WORLD OF GUMBALL MAD LIBS® • ™ & © TBS Europe Ltd, Cartoon Network. (s14).
Published in 2014 by Price Stern Sloan, an imprint of Penguin Random House LLC, 345 Hudson Street, New York, NY 10014.

MAD LIBS® is fun to play with friends, but you can also play it by yourself! To begin with, DO NOT look at the story on the page below. Fill in the blanks on this page with the words called for. Then, using the words you have selected, fill in the blank spaces in the story.

Now you've created your own hilarious MAD LIBS® game!

REPORT CARD

NOUN _____

NUMBER _____

NOUN _____

NOUN _____

NOUN _____

PLURAL NOUN _____

ADJECTIVE _____

PLURAL NOUN _____

ADJECTIVE _____

ADJECTIVE _____

VERB ENDING IN "ING" _____

ADJECTIVE _____

ADVERB _____

NOUN _____

MAD LIBS
REPORT CARD

Dear Mr. and Mrs. Watterson, here is Gumball's report card for this term.

Please sign and return within the next _____.

NOUN

- Times tardy: _____

NUMBER

- Arithmetic: struggles with _____-solving

NOUN

- Geography: has trouble finding any _____ on a map

NOUN

- Reading: makes up his _____ reports

NOUN

- History: has difficulty remembering names and _____

PLURAL NOUN

- Attitude toward schoolwork: needs to be more _____; school isn't

ADJECTIVE

  all fun and _____

PLURAL NOUN

- Conduct: totally _____, and it drives me _____!

ADJECTIVE   ADJECTIVE

- Other comments: Gumball shows interest in school, but that interest has

  to do with _____ in class and making _____

VERB ENDING IN "ING"   ADJECTIVE

  excuses for forgetting his homework. Therefore I _____ recommend

ADVERB

  that Gumball attend _____ school.

NOUN

Sincerely,

Miss Simian

From THE AMAZING WORLD OF GUMBALL MAD LIBS® • ™ & © TBS Europe Ltd, Cartoon Network. (s14).
Published in 2014 by Price Stern Sloan, an imprint of Penguin Random House LLC, 345 Hudson Street, New York, NY 10014.

MAD LIBS® is fun to play with friends, but you can also play it by yourself! To begin with, DO NOT look at the story on the page below. Fill in the blanks on this page with the words called for. Then, using the words you have selected, fill in the blank spaces in the story.

Now you've created your own hilarious MAD LIBS® game!

FOREST OF DOOM

EXCLAMATION _____

NOUN _____

NOUN _____

ADJECTIVE _____

ADJECTIVE _____

ADVERB _____

VERB ENDING IN "ING" _____

PLURAL NOUN _____

NOUN _____

ADJECTIVE _____

PLURAL NOUN _____

PART OF THE BODY (PLURAL) _____

ADJECTIVE _____

ADJECTIVE _____

NOUN _____

MAD LIBS

FOREST OF DOOM

_____! Whatever you do, do not go into the _____ of Doom.
　　EXCLAMATION　　　　　　　　　　　　　　　　　　　NOUN

Located in the middle of the _____ in Elmore, it might look totally
　　　　　　　　　　　　　　　NOUN

_____, but when viewed from above, it possesses a/an _____
ADJECTIVE　　　　　　　　　　　　　　　　　　　　　　　ADJECTIVE

resemblance to a human skull. It's also _____ dark in the forest, even
　　　　　　　　　　　　　　　　　　　　ADVERB

when the sun is _____, because the _____ are so
　　　　　　VERB ENDING IN "ING"　　　　　　　　PLURAL NOUN

tall and thick that they block the sunlight. The forest is bigger than it looks

from the outside, and it is easy to lose your _____ inside. The forest is
　　　　　　　　　　　　　　　　　　　　　　　NOUN

home to a variety of _____ plants and _____—there are
　　　　　　　　　　　ADJECTIVE　　　　　　　PLURAL NOUN

trees with snarling _____, monstrous squirrels,
　　　　　　　　　PART OF THE BODY (PLURAL)

_____ chicken-deer hybrids, and some _____ monsters. So
ADJECTIVE　　　　　　　　　　　　　　　　ADJECTIVE

it's no surprise that Gumball and Darwin managed to get themselves lost in the

_____ . . .
　NOUN

From THE AMAZING WORLD OF GUMBALL MAD LIBS® • ™ & © TBS Europe Ltd, Cartoon Network. (s14).
Published in 2014 by Price Stern Sloan, an imprint of Penguin Random House LLC, 345 Hudson Street, New York, NY 10014.

MAD LIBS® is fun to play with friends, but you can also play it by yourself! To begin with, DO NOT look at the story on the page below. Fill in the blanks on this page with the words called for. Then, using the words you have selected, fill in the blank spaces in the story.

Now you've created your own hilarious MAD LIBS® game!

MY LITTLE ONES, BY RICHARD WATTERSON

NOUN _____

PLURAL NOUN _____

ADJECTIVE _____

NOUN _____

ADVERB _____

NOUN _____

VERB (PAST TENSE) _____

NOUN _____

VERB _____

NOUN _____

VERB _____

ADJECTIVE _____

PLURAL NOUN _____

VERB _____

SAME VERB _____

NOUN _____

ADJECTIVE _____

MAD LIBS®
MY LITTLE ONES,
BY RICHARD WATTERSON

I would like to dedicate this _____ to my _____:
_____NOUN_____ _____PLURAL NOUN_____

I remember when you were still _____, my little ones.
_____ADJECTIVE_____

I was the _____ who picked you up when you fell _____.
_____NOUN_____ _____ADVERB_____

And life was just one funny _____, my little ones.
_____NOUN_____

We _____ every day as the world went around.
_____VERB (PAST TENSE)_____

I was the _____ who taught you how to _____.
_____NOUN_____ _____VERB_____

I was the _____ who taught you how to _____.
_____NOUN_____ _____VERB_____

And now you're no longer so _____, my little _____.
_____ADJECTIVE_____ _____PLURAL NOUN_____

You'll _____ so much more than I ever will _____.
_____VERB_____ _____SAME VERB_____

And though I'm just Dad, not a/an _____, my little ones,
_____NOUN_____

being just Dad is _____ enough for me.
_____ADJECTIVE_____

MAD LIBS® is fun to play with friends, but you can also play it by yourself! To begin with, DO NOT look at the story on the page below. Fill in the blanks on this page with the words called for. Then, using the words you have selected, fill in the blank spaces in the story.

Now you've created your own hilarious MAD LIBS® game!

WELCOME TO ELMORE!

ADJECTIVE _____

VERB ENDING IN "ING" _____

NOUN _____

NOUN _____

ADJECTIVE _____

PLURAL NOUN _____

NOUN _____

PLURAL NOUN _____

NOUN _____

ADJECTIVE _____

NOUN _____

ADJECTIVE _____

MAD LIBS

WELCOME TO ELMORE!

Let's take a tour of the _____ town of Elmore. It's just like any small
        ADJECTIVE

town in America. It has a mall, where the Wattersons do a lot of their

_____. There is a state-of-the-_____ hospital, where
VERB ENDING IN "ING"   NOUN

Gumball was treated after falling off a/an _____ on the Elmore
                                            NOUN

Expressway. There's the junkyard, which can sometimes be a/an _____
                                                              ADJECTIVE

place to find _____ for a date. Two of Gumball and Darwin's
              PLURAL NOUN

favorite places in Elmore are Ripley 2000 (the _____-game store) and
                                                NOUN

Laser Video, where they rent their favorite _____. An important
                                            PLURAL NOUN

part of Elmore's _____ is Chanax Inc. (although no one is sure just
                  NOUN

what goes on inside the building). And of course there is Elmore Junior High

School, where Gumball, Darwin, and Anais are all _____ students.
                                                  ADJECTIVE

Last but not least, there is the cute blue _____ where the
                                            NOUN

_____ Watterson family lives. We hope you enjoy your stay!
ADJECTIVE

From THE AMAZING WORLD OF GUMBALL MAD LIBS® • ™ & © TBS Europe Ltd, Cartoon Network. (s14).
Published in 2014 by Price Stern Sloan, an imprint of Penguin Random House LLC, 345 Hudson Street, New York, NY 10014.

MAD LIBS® is fun to play with friends, but you can also play it by yourself! To begin with, DO NOT look at the story on the page below. Fill in the blanks on this page with the words called for. Then, using the words you have selected, fill in the blank spaces in the story.

Now you've created your own hilarious MAD LIBS® game!

SAVE CHRISTMAS!

TYPE OF VEHICLE _____

NOUN _____

ADJECTIVE _____

NOUN _____

ADJECTIVE _____

PERSON IN ROOM (FEMALE) _____

PERSON IN ROOM (MALE) _____

ADJECTIVE _____

NOUN _____

ADJECTIVE _____

PLURAL NOUN _____

VERB ENDING IN "ING" _____

NOUN _____

MAD LIBS
SAVE CHRISTMAS!

Leave it to the Wattersons to hit Santa with their _____! And
                                                    TYPE OF VEHICLE

because Richard is such a worry-_____, he's sure it will land the entire
                                  NOUN

family on Santa's _____ list. But it turns out that Santa is actually a
                   ADJECTIVE

homeless _____! The doctor tells Richard that they have a/an
          NOUN

_____ obligation to look after him. _____ objects,
 ADJECTIVE   PERSON IN ROOM (FEMALE)

but of course Gumball, _____, and Anais plead with their
                        PERSON IN ROOM (MALE)

parents to let "Santa" come home with them. So Richard agrees, because maybe

Christmas *can* be saved! But of course nothing is ever _____ in the
                                                         ADJECTIVE

Watterson _____-hold, and their good deed turns into a/an
           NOUN

_____ disaster. However, with some Christmas _____
 ADJECTIVE   PLURAL NOUN

and a lot of _____, the Wattersons do save the _____.
              VERB ENDING IN "ING"   NOUN

Can't wait for Easter!

From THE AMAZING WORLD OF GUMBALL MAD LIBS® • ™ & © TBS Europe Ltd, Cartoon Network. (s14). Published in
2014 by Price Stern Sloan, an imprint of Penguin Random House LLC, 345 Hudson Street,
New York, NY 10014.

FIONNA & CAKE
MAD LIBS®

PSS!
PRICE STERN SLOAN
An Imprint of Penguin Random House

INSTRUCTIONS

MAD LIBS® is a game for people who don't like games!
It can be played by one, two, three, four, or forty.

• RIDICULOUSLY SIMPLE DIRECTIONS

In this tablet you will find stories containing blank spaces where words are left out. One player, the READER, selects one of these stories. The READER does not tell anyone what the story is about. Instead, he/she asks the other players, the WRITERS, to give him/her words. These words are used to fill in the blank spaces in the story.

• TO PLAY

The READER asks each WRITER in turn to call out a word—an adjective or a noun or whatever the space calls for—and uses them to fill in the blank spaces in the story. The result is a MAD LIBS® game.

When the READER then reads the completed MAD LIBS® game to the other players, they will discover that they have written a story that is fantastic, screamingly funny, shocking, silly, crazy, or just plain dumb—depending upon which words each WRITER called out.

• EXAMPLE (*Before* and *After*)

"_____!" he said _____
       EXCLAMATION   ADVERB

as he jumped into his convertible _____ and
                                      NOUN

drove off with his _____ wife.
                    ADJECTIVE

"_____OUCH_____!" he said _____STUPIDLY_____
       EXCLAMATION   ADVERB

as he jumped into his convertible _____CAT_____ and
                                      NOUN

drove off with his _____BRAVE_____ wife.
                    ADJECTIVE

QUICK REVIEW

In case you have forgotten what adjectives, adverbs, nouns, and verbs are, here is a quick review:

An ADJECTIVE describes something or somebody. *Lumpy, soft, ugly, messy,* and *short* are adjectives.

An ADVERB tells how something is done. It modifies a verb and usually ends in "ly." *Modestly, stupidly, greedily,* and *carefully* are adverbs.

A NOUN is the name of a person, place, or thing. *Sidewalk, umbrella, bridle, bathtub,* and *nose* are nouns.

A VERB is an action word. *Run, pitch, jump,* and *swim* are verbs. Put the verbs in past tense if the directions say PAST TENSE. *Ran, pitched, jumped,* and *swam* are verbs in the past tense.

When we ask for A PLACE, we mean any sort of place: a country or city *(Spain, Cleveland)* or a room *(bathroom, kitchen).*

An EXCLAMATION or SILLY WORD is any sort of funny sound, gasp, grunt, or outcry, like *Wow!, Ouch!, Whomp!, Ick!,* and *Gadzooks!*

When we ask for specific words, like a NUMBER, a COLOR, an ANIMAL, or a PART OF THE BODY, we mean a word that is one of those things, like *seven, blue, horse,* or *head.*

When we ask for a PLURAL, it means more than one. For example, *cat* pluralized is *cats.*

MAD LIBS® is fun to play with friends, but you can also play it by yourself! To begin with, DO NOT look at the story on the page below. Fill in the blanks on this page with the words called for. Then, using the words you have selected, fill in the blank spaces in the story.

Now you've created your own hilarious MAD LIBS® game!

CAKE THE CAT AND FIONNA THE HUMAN

PART OF THE BODY _____

NOUN _____

NOUN _____

ADJECTIVE _____

PLURAL NOUN _____

TYPE OF FOOD _____

ADJECTIVE _____

SILLY WORD _____

PLURAL NOUN _____

NOUN _____

ADJECTIVE _____

ADJECTIVE _____

PERSON IN ROOM (MALE) _____

NOUN _____

SILLY WORD _____

NOUN _____

MAD LIBS®
CAKE THE CAT AND
FIONNA THE HUMAN

Fionna is a super awesome, _____-kicking human girl who loves
                          PART OF THE BODY

weapons and is as tough and strong as a/an _____. Her best
                                            NOUN

_____ forever is Cake the _____-tongued, shape-shifting
   NOUN   ADJECTIVE

cat. These two _____ are inseparable. They go together like peanut
               PLURAL NOUN

butter and _____. Fionna and Cake live together in a/an
           TYPE OF FOOD

_____ tree house in the land of _____, where, together, they
  ADJECTIVE   SILLY WORD

fight bad _____, save princes from the clutches of the evil Ice
          PLURAL NOUN

_____, and go on _____ adventures. Fionna has a/an
    NOUN   ADJECTIVE

_____ crush on Prince _____, which is perfect because
  ADJECTIVE   PERSON IN ROOM (MALE)

Cake loves the prince's loyal _____, Lord _____. The
                             NOUN   SILLY WORD

_____ never stops with Fionna and Cake!
   NOUN

MAD LIBS® is fun to play with friends, but you can also play it by yourself! To begin with, DO NOT look at the story on the page below. Fill in the blanks on this page with the words called for. Then, using the words you have selected, fill in the blank spaces in the story.

Now you've created your own hilarious MAD LIBS® game!

PRINCE GUMBALL
REIGNS SUPREME

ADJECTIVE _____

ADJECTIVE _____

PLURAL NOUN _____

ADJECTIVE _____

PART OF THE BODY _____

ADJECTIVE _____

ADJECTIVE _____

ADJECTIVE _____

PART OF THE BODY _____

ADJECTIVE _____

NOUN _____

TYPE OF LIQUID _____

PLURAL NOUN _____

NOUN _____

NOUN _____

MAD LIBS®
PRINCE GUMBALL
REIGNS SUPREME

Welcome, visitor, to the _____ Candy Kingdom. I, the _____
         ADJECTIVE   ADJECTIVE

Prince Gumball, rule over my subjects, the Candy _____, with
                                                  PLURAL NOUN

a/an _____ heart and a kind _____. I think you'll find
      ADJECTIVE   PART OF THE BODY

the citizens of the Candy Kingdom to be _____, _____
                                         ADJECTIVE   ADJECTIVE

hosts. (Just don't try to eat the talking candy, or the _____ Gumball
                                                         ADJECTIVE

Guardians will kick you out of these castle walls so fast, your _____
                                                                PART OF THE BODY

will spin.) While you're here, I hope you'll take a/an _____ stroll
                                                       ADJECTIVE

down the peanut brittle _____ or go for a dip in the _____
                         NOUN   TYPE OF LIQUID

river. Though I recommend you stay away from the Candy Tavern—you never

know what manner of _____ you'll find there. But I'm sure you'll
                     PLURAL NOUN

find that the Candy Kingdom is as sweet as a sugary _____. Do enjoy
                                                     NOUN

your _____!
      NOUN

From FIONNA AND CAKE MAD LIBS® • ™ & © Cartoon Network. (s13). Published in 2013 by
Price Stern Sloan, an imprint of Penguin Random House LLC, 345 Hudson Street, New York, NY 10014.

MAD LIBS® is fun to play with friends, but you can also play it by yourself! To begin with, DO NOT look at the story on the page below. Fill in the blanks on this page with the words called for. Then, using the words you have selected, fill in the blank spaces in the story.

Now you've created your own hilarious MAD LIBS® game!

YOU'RE INVITED TO THE GUMBALL BALL

PERSON IN ROOM _____

NOUN _____

A PLACE _____

ADVERB _____

NOUN _____

TYPE OF FOOD _____

NOUN _____

NUMBER _____

PERSON IN ROOM (MALE) _____

ADVERB _____

NOUN _____

VERB ENDING IN "ING" _____

ADJECTIVE _____

PLURAL NOUN _____

CELEBRITY _____

NOUN _____

VERB _____

MAD LIBS®
YOU'RE INVITED TO
THE GUMBALL BALL

Dear _____, distinguished _____ of (the) _____,
_____PERSON IN ROOM_____   _____NOUN_____   _____A PLACE_____

You are _____ invited to the first annual Gumball
       _____ADVERB_____

_____, held in the _____ Ballroom at the
_____NOUN_____   _____TYPE OF FOOD_____

_____ Castle this Saturday at _____ o'clock in the evening.
_____NOUN_____   _____NUMBER_____

Prince _____ himself has _____ requested your
      _____PERSON IN ROOM (MALE)_____   _____ADVERB_____

presence as his special _____ of honor. There will be dancing, eating,
       _____NOUN_____

and _____, with entertainment provided by the _____
    _____VERB ENDING IN "ING"_____   _____ADJECTIVE_____

rock band the Devil Cake _____, with a special guest appearance by
       _____PLURAL NOUN_____

_____. Dress attire is formal, so please wear your finest _____
_____CELEBRITY_____   _____NOUN_____

and be prepared to _____ the night away.
       _____VERB_____

From FIONNA AND CAKE MAD LIBS® • ™ & © Cartoon Network. (s13). Published in 2013 by
Price Stern Sloan, an imprint of Penguin Random House LLC, 345 Hudson Street, New York, NY 10014.

MAD LIBS® is fun to play with friends, but you can also play it by yourself! To begin with, DO NOT look at the story on the page below. Fill in the blanks on this page with the words called for. Then, using the words you have selected, fill in the blank spaces in the story.

Now you've created your own hilarious MAD LIBS® game!

IS IT A DATE?

ADJECTIVE _____

NOUN _____

NOUN _____

ADJECTIVE _____

VERB _____

ADJECTIVE _____

NOUN _____

NOUN _____

NOUN _____

ADJECTIVE _____

ADJECTIVE _____

PLURAL NOUN _____

PLURAL NOUN _____

ADJECTIVE _____

VERB _____

ADJECTIVE _____

After Fionna saved Prince Gumball from the _____ Ice Queen, he
                                              ADJECTIVE

asked Fionna to go out. But when a/an _____ you like asks you to
                                          NOUN

hang out, it can sometimes be difficult to tell whether it's a date or just a/an

_____ between friends. How can you be sure? Just ask yourself these
   NOUN

_____ questions:
   ADJECTIVE

• Did you agree on a time and place to _____ in advance? If,
                                            VERB

   so, it's a/an _____ date.
                   ADJECTIVE

• When you show up, does the other _____ compliment your
                                        NOUN

   _____ or give you a/an _____ as a present? If so, it's
      NOUN   NOUN

   a/an _____ date.
           ADJECTIVE

• Does the other person serenade you with a/an _____
                                                    ADJECTIVE

   song about _____ and _____? If so, it's a/an
                 PLURAL NOUN   PLURAL NOUN

   _____ date.
      ADJECTIVE

• Does the other person say "I _____ you" at the end of the
                                    VERB

   night? If so, it's a/an _____ date.
                              ADJECTIVE

MAD LIBS® is fun to play with friends, but you can also play it by yourself! To begin with, DO NOT look at the story on the page below. Fill in the blanks on this page with the words called for. Then, using the words you have selected, fill in the blank spaces in the story.

Now you've created your own hilarious MAD LIBS® game!

FINN VS. FIONNA

PLURAL NOUN _____

NOUN _____

SILLY WORD _____

PLURAL NOUN _____

PLURAL NOUN _____

VERB _____

PLURAL NOUN _____

NOUN _____

TYPE OF FOOD _____

NOUN _____

NOUN _____

NOUN _____

NOUN _____

NOUN _____

NOUN _____

Fionna is the girl version of Finn, so naturally, the two have many

_____ in common. They are each the only remaining
PLURAL NOUN

_____ in the Land of _____. They both enjoy fighting
NOUN   SILLY WORD

with swords made of _____. They are both fearless _____
PLURAL NOUN   PLURAL NOUN

who love to _____. But how are these two _____ different
VERB   PLURAL NOUN

from each other? Well, first of all, Finn kind of has a thing for Princess

Bubble-_____, while Fionna sort of likes Prince _____.
NOUN   TYPE OF FOOD

Finn's best _____ is Jake the _____, and Fionna's best
NOUN   NOUN

_____ is Cake the _____. But of course, the major difference
NOUN   NOUN

between Finn and Fionna is that Finn is a real _____ and Fionna only
NOUN

exists in the _____ King's fan fiction!
NOUN

From FIONNA AND CAKE MAD LIBS® • ™ & © Cartoon Network. (s13). Published in 2013 by
Price Stern Sloan, an imprint of Penguin Random House LLC, 345 Hudson Street, New York, NY 10014.

MAD LIBS® is fun to play with friends, but you can also play it by yourself! To begin with, DO NOT look at the story on the page below. Fill in the blanks on this page with the words called for. Then, using the words you have selected, fill in the blank spaces in the story.

Now you've created your own hilarious MAD LIBS® game!

ICE QUEEN
HEARTS PRINCES

ADJECTIVE _____

ADJECTIVE _____

ADJECTIVE _____

ADJECTIVE _____

ADJECTIVE _____

PLURAL NOUN _____

ADVERB _____

TYPE OF CLOTHING _____

PLURAL NOUN _____

NOUN _____

ADJECTIVE _____

A PLACE _____

ADVERB _____

ADJECTIVE _____

ADVERB _____

That _____ tomboy Fionna says I like to predator on
     ADJECTIVE

_____ dudes. But not just any dudes—I love princes.
    ADJECTIVE

_____ princes, _____ princes, _____
  ADJECTIVE   ADJECTIVE   ADJECTIVE

princes—any prince will do. Why do I like these royal _____ so
                                       PLURAL NOUN

much? Well . . .

Princes always dress so _____, in their fancy _____ and
                  ADVERB   TYPE OF CLOTHING

their sparkly crowns made of _____.
                       PLURAL NOUN

Princes are so chivalrous and gentlemanly—they really know how to treat a/an

_____.
  NOUN

Princes throw the most _____ parties and balls in all of (the)
                   ADJECTIVE

_____.
  A PLACE

Princes rule _____ over their kingdoms and they have lots of
          ADVERB

_____ power.
  ADJECTIVE

Princes are just _____ cute, okay?
           ADVERB

From FIONNA AND CAKE MAD LIBS® • ™ & © Cartoon Network. (s13). Published in 2013 by
Price Stern Sloan, an imprint of Penguin Random House LLC, 345 Hudson Street, New York, NY 10014.

MAD LIBS® is fun to play with friends, but you can also play it by yourself! To begin with, DO NOT look at the story on the page below. Fill in the blanks on this page with the words called for. Then, using the words you have selected, fill in the blank spaces in the story.

Now you've created your own hilarious MAD LIBS® game!

TRUSTY LORD MONOCHROMICORN

NOUN _____

A PLACE _____

NOUN _____

COLOR _____

PART OF THE BODY _____

ADJECTIVE _____

ADJECTIVE _____

PART OF THE BODY _____

PLURAL NOUN _____

PERSON IN ROOM _____

NOUN _____

ADJECTIVE _____

PART OF THE BODY (PLURAL) _____

NOUN _____

MAD LIBS®
TRUSTY LORD
MONOCHROMICORN

Lord Monochromicorn is Prince Gumball's trusty steed and his best

_____ in (the) _____. Part unicorn, part
     NOUN   A PLACE

_____, Lord Monochromicorn—or Mo-Chro, as Prince Gumball
     NOUN

calls him—has a long _____ mane and sleek black hair covering his
                              COLOR

entire _____. His horn is _____, and his eyes glow a/an
        PART OF THE BODY   ADJECTIVE

_____ white. Lord Monochromicorn speaks by scratching his
    ADJECTIVE

_____ on the ground, which is confusing for _____ who
 PART OF THE BODY   PLURAL NOUN

don't understand _____ code. Luckily, Cake the _____
                   PERSON IN ROOM   NOUN

does—and Cake has a/an _____ crush on Mo-Chro and thinks
                            ADJECTIVE

he's the bee's _____. Luckily, Mo-Chro thinks Cake is the
                PART OF THE BODY (PLURAL)

_____'s pajamas, too!
     NOUN

From FIONNA AND CAKE MAD LIBS® • ™ & © Cartoon Network. (s13). Published in 2013 by
Price Stern Sloan, an imprint of Penguin Random House LLC, 345 Hudson Street, New York, NY 10014.

MAD LIBS® is fun to play with friends, but you can also play it by yourself! To begin with, DO NOT look at the story on the page below. Fill in the blanks on this page with the words called for. Then, using the words you have selected, fill in the blank spaces in the story.

Now you've created your own hilarious MAD LIBS® game!

PRINCE GUMBALL'S OTHER SUBJECTS

PLURAL NOUN _____

ADJECTIVE _____

NOUN _____

NUMBER _____

PLURAL NOUN _____

NOUN _____

PLURAL NOUN _____

PART OF THE BODY (PLURAL) _____

COLOR _____

PART OF THE BODY _____

ADJECTIVE _____

ADJECTIVE _____

NOUN _____

PERSON IN ROOM (FEMALE) _____

MAD LIBS®
PRINCE GUMBALL'S
OTHER SUBJECTS

You've met Fionna, Cake, the Ice Queen, and Lord Monochromicorn—but

who are the other _____ who live in Prince Gumball's _____
                        PLURAL NOUN   ADJECTIVE

kingdom? Here are a few of them:

Marshall Lee—Marshall Lee is one rock 'n' roll _____. This vampire
                                                         NOUN

dude is over _____ years old and isn't scared of any _____.
                 NUMBER   PLURAL NOUN

Ms. Cinnamon Bun—This doughy _____ has a few loose
                                      NOUN

_____ and is not very graceful on her _____, though
  PLURAL NOUN   PART OF THE BODY (PLURAL)

she sure looks pretty in a/an _____ dress with a bow on her _____.
                                  COLOR   PART OF THE BODY

Ms. Starchy—Poor Ms. Starchy has a/an _____ mustache. It's very
                                               ADJECTIVE

unbecoming on a/an _____ lady such as herself!
                        ADJECTIVE

Lumpy Space Prince—This blobby purple _____ can't stop talking
                                               NOUN

about his girlfriend, _____.
                       PERSON IN ROOM (FEMALE)

From FIONNA AND CAKE MAD LIBS® • ™ & © Cartoon Network. (s13). Published in 2013 by
Price Stern Sloan, an imprint of Penguin Random House LLC, 345 Hudson Street, New York, NY 10014.

MAD LIBS® is fun to play with friends, but you can also play it by yourself! To begin with, DO NOT look at the story on the page below. Fill in the blanks on this page with the words called for. Then, using the words you have selected, fill in the blank spaces in the story.

Now you've created your own hilarious MAD LIBS® game!

CAKE'S DATING ADVICE

NOUN _____

ADJECTIVE _____

NOUN _____

ADJECTIVE _____

NOUN _____

PART OF THE BODY (PLURAL) _____

NOUN _____

PLURAL NOUN _____

PLURAL NOUN _____

ADJECTIVE _____

PLURAL NOUN _____

ADJECTIVE _____

ANIMAL _____

ADJECTIVE _____

ADJECTIVE _____

SILLY WORD _____

PART OF THE BODY _____

PART OF THE BODY _____

MAD LIBS®
CAKE'S DATING ADVICE

Hello, gorgeous _____! Got a/an _____ date and want them
                        NOUN   ADJECTIVE

to be impressed with your _____? Just follow my _____
                              NOUN   ADJECTIVE

advice, and your _____ will fall head over _____ for
                        NOUN   PART OF THE BODY (PLURAL)

your sweet _____!
                NOUN

• Tell your date he or she is hot. _____ *love* hearing
                                        PLURAL NOUN

  that they're hot!

• Act interested in your date's _____, even if they're
                                      PLURAL NOUN

  _____. Then they'll think your _____ are
        ADJECTIVE   PLURAL NOUN

  interesting, too!

• Laugh so loudly at your date's _____ jokes that you snort like
                                      ADJECTIVE

  a/an _____.
          ANIMAL

• If you really like your _____ date, make your tail all
                              ADJECTIVE

  _____ and fluffy, like I do when I see Lord _____.
    ADJECTIVE   SILLY WORD

  Don't have a/an _____? Just wag your _____ at
                      PART OF THE BODY   PART OF THE BODY

  them instead!

MAD LIBS® is fun to play with friends, but you can also play it by yourself! To begin with, DO NOT look at the story on the page below. Fill in the blanks on this page with the words called for. Then, using the words you have selected, fill in the blank spaces in the story.

Now you've created your own hilarious MAD LIBS® game!

JAKE VS. CAKE

NOUN _____

NOUN _____

PART OF THE BODY (PLURAL) _____

NOUN _____

NOUN _____

ADJECTIVE _____

NOUN _____

COLOR _____

PART OF THE BODY (PLURAL) _____

COLOR _____

PART OF THE BODY _____

NOUN _____

NOUN _____

ADJECTIVE _____

NOUN _____

SILLY WORD _____

ADJECTIVE _____

PART OF THE BODY _____

MAD LIBS®
JAKE VS. CAKE

Jake the dog is Finn's best _____ in the world, and Cake the cat is
                                    NOUN

Fionna's right-hand _____. While they both can morph their
                            NOUN

_____ into a/an _____ at a moment's notice, Jake
PART OF THE BODY (PLURAL)   NOUN

and Cake are like night and _____. First of all, Jake and Cake are
                                    NOUN

different species! Jake is a/an _____ dog, while Cake is
                                        ADJECTIVE

a/an _____. Jake is bright _____ with droopy
            NOUN   COLOR

_____, while Cake is white and _____ with a
PART OF THE BODY (PLURAL)   COLOR

big, bushy _____. Jake plays the viola, but Cake prefers to strum
                PART OF THE BODY

the _____. Jake loves Princess _____'s companion,
        NOUN   NOUN

Lady Rainicorn, but Cake is _____ for Prince _____'s pal
                                    ADJECTIVE   NOUN

Lord _____. But when you put Jake and Cake's differences aside, it
        SILLY WORD

becomes clear that they share one very _____ similarity—they always
                                                ADJECTIVE

have their best friends' interests at _____.
                                        PART OF THE BODY

MAD LIBS® is fun to play with friends, but you can also play it by yourself! To begin with, DO NOT look at the story on the page below. Fill in the blanks on this page with the words called for. Then, using the words you have selected, fill in the blank spaces in the story.

Now you've created your own hilarious MAD LIBS® game!

HOW TO WOO FIONNA

PLURAL NOUN _____

PART OF THE BODY _____

PLURAL NOUN _____

ADJECTIVE _____

NOUN _____

ADJECTIVE _____

PLURAL NOUN _____

ADJECTIVE _____

NOUN _____

PLURAL NOUN _____

ADJECTIVE _____

TYPE OF LIQUID _____

VERB ENDING IN "ING" _____

ADJECTIVE _____

A PLACE _____

PLURAL NOUN _____

MAD LIBS®
HOW TO WOO FIONNA

Fionna's not like other _____. The way to her _____ isn't
             PLURAL NOUN   PART OF THE BODY

through romantic _____ or _____ gestures. No. Fionna is
             PLURAL NOUN   ADJECTIVE

one tough and adventurous _____. If you want to win over Fionna,
                      NOUN

you have to think like Fionna. Here are some _____ tips:
                                 ADJECTIVE

DON'T give her a pretty bouquet of _____. Bo-ring.
                            PLURAL NOUN

DO give her a/an _____ weapon, such as a crystal _____
              ADJECTIVE   NOUN

or a pair of nunchakus made out of _____.
                          PLURAL NOUN

DON'T take her to a/an _____ restaurant for a candlelit dinner and
                  ADJECTIVE

glasses of fancy _____.
           TYPE OF LIQUID

DO take her _____ in the _____ cliffs of (the)
         VERB ENDING IN "ING"   ADJECTIVE

_____, seeking out bad guys and evil _____.
  A PLACE   PLURAL NOUN

MAD LIBS® is fun to play with friends, but you can also play it by yourself! To begin with, DO NOT look at the story on the page below. Fill in the blanks on this page with the words called for. Then, using the words you have selected, fill in the blank spaces in the story.

Now you've created your own hilarious MAD LIBS® game!

A DREAM COME TRUE, BY FIONNA

NOUN _____

NOUN _____

PLURAL NOUN _____

NOUN _____

PLURAL NOUN _____

PART OF THE BODY _____

PART OF THE BODY _____

SAME PART OF THE BODY _____

ANIMAL _____

PART OF THE BODY (PLURAL) _____

PART OF THE BODY _____

ADJECTIVE _____

NOUN _____

PART OF THE BODY _____

ADJECTIVE _____

ADJECTIVE _____

EXCLAMATION _____

MAD LIBS®
A DREAM COME TRUE, BY FIONNA

Oh, Cake! My date with Prince Gumball was out of this _____! Not

NOUN

only did he think to bring me a crystal _____ disguised in a bouquet

NOUN

of _____, he also brought you a satchel of _____-nip.

PLURAL NOUN _NOUN_

Wow. Our race to the Marshmallow _____ got my _____

PLURAL NOUN _PART OF THE BODY_

racing. And I totally kicked his _____. (Not that I was thinking of his

PART OF THE BODY

_____.) When he said he found a pearl _____ skull

SAME PART OF THE BODY _ANIMAL_

and that it reminded him of my sparkly _____, I thought my

PART OF THE BODY (PLURAL)

_____ might explode. Then he sang me a/an _____ song,

PART OF THE BODY _ADJECTIVE_

and even though I said it was the stupidest _____ ever, I loved it with

NOUN

all my _____. Then we lay in the grass and told each other our deepest,

PART OF THE BODY

most _____ secrets. Then he asked me to go to the ball with him, _as_

ADJECTIVE

his _____ _girlfriend_! _____! It was awesome.

ADJECTIVE _EXCLAMATION_

MAD LIBS® is fun to play with friends, but you can also play it by yourself! To begin with, DO NOT look at the story on the page below. Fill in the blanks on this page with the words called for. Then, using the words you have selected, fill in the blank spaces in the story.

Now you've created your own hilarious MAD LIBS® game!

PRINCE GUMBALL'S SERENADE

ADJECTIVE _____

ADVERB _____

NOUN _____

ADJECTIVE _____

ADJECTIVE _____

VERB _____

ADJECTIVE _____

NOUN _____

VERB _____

PERSON IN ROOM _____

PART OF THE BODY _____

SAME PERSON IN ROOM _____

NOUN _____

MAD LIBS®
PRINCE GUMBALL'S
SERENADE

During their date, Prince Gumball sang a/an _____ song to Fionna
                                              ADJECTIVE

while Cake _____ strummed his dulcimer. It was a/an _____
              ADVERB   NOUN

for the ages. Here are the _____ lyrics:
                              ADJECTIVE

I feel like nothing was _____ until I met you.
                            ADJECTIVE

I feel like we really _____, and I really get you.
                          VERB

If I said you're a/an _____ _____, would it upset you?
                          ADJECTIVE   NOUN

Because the way you _____ tonight,
                        VERB

Silhouetted, I'll never forget it.

Oh, oh, _____.
            PERSON IN ROOM

Your _____ has touched my heart.
         PART OF THE BODY

Oh, oh, _____.
            SAME PERSON IN ROOM

I won't let anything in this _____ keep us apart.
                                  NOUN

MAD LIBS® is fun to play with friends, but you can also play it by yourself! To begin with, DO NOT look at the story on the page below. Fill in the blanks on this page with the words called for. Then, using the words you have selected, fill in the blank spaces in the story.

Now you've created your own hilarious MAD LIBS® game!

GETTING READY
FOR THE BALL

PLURAL NOUN _____

ADJECTIVE _____

ADVERB _____

NOUN _____

VERB (PAST TENSE) _____

NOUN _____

NOUN _____

ARTICLE OF CLOTHING _____

PLURAL NOUN _____

ADVERB _____

ADJECTIVE _____

NOUN _____

ADJECTIVE _____

ADVERB _____

NOUN _____

NOUN _____

MAD LIBS®
GETTING READY
FOR THE BALL

"Oh, my _____, it's almost seven!" Cake said to Fionna. Sure enough,
                 PLURAL NOUN

the _____ Gumball Ball was _____ approaching, and Fionna
        ADJECTIVE   ADVERB

wasn't ready. "Oh, hold on, _____, I'm gonna make this happen!"
                                    NOUN

said Cake, as she _____ around like a/an _____ on
                        VERB (PAST TENSE)   NOUN

fire. "Here, honey, put on this _____." Cake handed Fionna a
                                        NOUN

white _____ decorated with gold _____.
           ARTICLE OF CLOTHING   PLURAL NOUN

Fionna _____ put it on. It was far too _____ for her taste,
              ADVERB   ADJECTIVE

but she looked beautiful. "You shine up like a new _____!" said Cake,
                                                          NOUN

handing her a small satchel. "How am I supposed to fit my _____
                                                                   ADJECTIVE

weapons in this?" asked Fionna. "It's a ball! You don't need weapons," Cake

said _____. But Fionna packed her retractable _____
          ADVERB   NOUN

anyway. "Okay, let's go!" said Cake. The party was about to begin, and Fionna

was sure to be the belle of the _____!
                                       NOUN

From FIONNA AND CAKE MAD LIBS® • ™ & © Cartoon Network. (s13). Published in 2013 by
Price Stern Sloan, an imprint of Penguin Random House LLC, 345 Hudson Street, New York, NY 10014.

MAD LIBS® is fun to play with friends, but you can also play it by yourself! To begin with, DO NOT look at the story on the page below. Fill in the blanks on this page with the words called for. Then, using the words you have selected, fill in the blank spaces in the story.

Now you've created your own hilarious MAD LIBS® game!

AT THE GUMBALL BALL

ADJECTIVE _____

PERSON IN ROOM (MALE) _____

VERB _____

SAME VERB (PAST TENSE) _____

PLURAL NOUN _____

NOUN _____

NOUN _____

COLOR _____

PLURAL NOUN _____

PLURAL NOUN _____

ADVERB _____

NOUN _____

PERSON IN ROOM _____

NOUN _____

PLURAL NOUN _____

ADVERB _____

NOUN _____

MAD LIBS

AT THE GUMBALL BALL

Candy Kingdom, Land of Ooo—The _____ party of the year took
                                              ADJECTIVE

place last night at the palace of Prince _____ Gumball. The
                                          PERSON IN ROOM (MALE)

Biennial Gumball Ball was the place to _____ and be
                                                        VERB

_____. The guest list was a who's who of Candy Kingdom
   SAME VERB (PAST TENSE)

_____. Attendees like Lumpy Space _____ and Ms.
   PLURAL NOUN   NOUN

Candy _____ floated down the _____ carpet, looking
          NOUN   COLOR

stunning in designer _____. The dance floor was filled with
                          PLURAL NOUN

_____ busting a move. All was going _____ until the ball
   PLURAL NOUN   ADVERB

was interrupted by a loud _____. "Party's over, everyone!" said
                               NOUN

_____. "The Ice _____ has just crashed the party." The
 PERSON IN ROOM   NOUN

room was filled with _____ of frustration as the guests _____
                        PLURAL NOUN   ADVERB

filed out of the party. But as one guest said, "Oh, well. There's always next

_____!"
   NOUN

From FIONNA AND CAKE MAD LIBS® • ™ & © Cartoon Network. (s13). Published in 2013 by
Price Stern Sloan, an imprint of Penguin Random House LLC, 345 Hudson Street, New York, NY 10014.

MAD LIBS® is fun to play with friends, but you can also play it by yourself! To begin with, DO NOT look at the story on the page below. Fill in the blanks on this page with the words called for. Then, using the words you have selected, fill in the blank spaces in the story.

Now you've created your own hilarious MAD LIBS® game!

THE BATTLE FOR GUMBALL

ADJECTIVE _____

NOUN _____

A PLACE _____

NOUN _____

NOUN _____

NOUN _____

NOUN _____

NOUN _____

ADJECTIVE _____

PART OF THE BODY (PLURAL) _____

PERSON IN ROOM _____

NOUN _____

PART OF THE BODY _____

PLURAL NOUN _____

NOUN _____

When Fionna and Cake arrive at the _____ Gumball Ball, Prince
_____(ADJECTIVE)

Gumball quickly whisks Fionna away. "I want to show you a/an

_____," he says, leading her up to (the) _____. Once
(NOUN)_____(A PLACE)

there, Fionna discovers the *real* Prince Gumball frozen in a/an _____
_____(NOUN)

on the ceiling! The Prince Gumball who led her there is a fake—worse, it's the

_____ Queen! "This is really messed up, Ice _____!" says
(NOUN)_____(NOUN)

Fionna. "What is your problem with my _____?" "You are the only
_____(NOUN)

_____ standing between me and Prince Gumball!" says the Ice Queen.
(NOUN)

Just then, Fionna remembers the _____ sword in her purse. But the
_____(ADJECTIVE)

sword turns into ice, trapping her _____! Fionna uses the ice
_____(PART OF THE BODY (PLURAL))

to release Prince _____ from his prison, then she knocks the Ice
_____(PERSON IN ROOM)

Queen's magic _____ off her head and gives the Ice Queen one last
_____(NOUN)

kick to the _____. "And that's for yanking my heart-_____!"
_____(PART OF THE BODY)_____(PLURAL NOUN)

she exclaims. And just like that, Fionna saves the _____!
_____(NOUN)

MAD LIBS® is fun to play with friends, but you can also play it by yourself! To begin with, DO NOT look at the story on the page below. Fill in the blanks on this page with the words called for. Then, using the words you have selected, fill in the blank spaces in the story.

Now you've created your own hilarious MAD LIBS® game!

WOE IS THE ICE QUEEN

PERSON IN ROOM _____

ADJECTIVE _____

NOUN _____

NOUN _____

A PLACE _____

ADJECTIVE _____

ADJECTIVE _____

NOUN _____

ADJECTIVE _____

PLURAL NOUN _____

VERB _____

NOUN _____

VERB _____

PERSON IN ROOM _____

ADJECTIVE _____

NOUN _____

MAD LIBS®
WOE IS THE ICE QUEEN

Oh, _____, my _____ penguin! Why is that _____
    PERSON IN ROOM   ADJECTIVE   NOUN

Fionna always _____-blocking my game? The only thing I want in
                    NOUN

all of (the) _____ is to marry a/an _____ prince. But nooo!
           A PLACE   ADJECTIVE

Fionna and that _____ cat, Cake, won't let me just kidnap one and
                ADJECTIVE

make him my _____! What does Fionna know about _____
           NOUN   ADJECTIVE

love, anyway? Does she just think two _____ are supposed to
                             PLURAL NOUN

_____ for each other naturally? How absurd! It's not like *she* has a
   VERB

boy-_____. So who is she to _____? Ugh. By
         NOUN   VERB

_____'s beard, my _____ penguin, one day I will have a
  PERSON IN ROOM   ADJECTIVE

prince to call my _____!
            NOUN

From FIONNA AND CAKE MAD LIBS® • ™ & © Cartoon Network. (s13). Published in 2013 by
Price Stern Sloan, an imprint of Penguin Random House LLC, 345 Hudson Street, New York, NY 10014.

MAD LIBS® is fun to play with friends, but you can also play it by yourself! To begin with, DO NOT look at the story on the page below. Fill in the blanks on this page with the words called for. Then, using the words you have selected, fill in the blank spaces in the story.

Now you've created your own hilarious MAD LIBS® game!

FIONNA'S
FAVORITE WEAPONS

ADJECTIVE _____

NOUN _____

NOUN _____

NOUN _____

ADJECTIVE _____

NOUN _____

ADJECTIVE _____

PLURAL NOUN _____

NOUN _____

NOUN _____

ADJECTIVE _____

NOUN _____

ADVERB _____

ADJECTIVE _____

NOUN _____

MAD LIBS®
FIONNA'S
FAVORITE WEAPONS

Fionna doesn't go anywhere without a/an _____ weapon tucked

ADJECTIVE

inside her _____. After all, in the Land of Ooo, danger could be

NOUN

lurking around any _____, and a girl has to be prepared for any

NOUN

_____! Her _____ sword is very practical: It's retractable, so

NOUN   ADJECTIVE

she can carry it inside a small _____ and no one will ever know. She is

NOUN

also a/an _____ shot with her bow and _____. But her best

ADJECTIVE   PLURAL NOUN

weapon is her _____, Cake! That's right. Cake can shift into any

NOUN

_____ Fionna needs, like a/an _____ star or a spiked

NOUN   ADJECTIVE

_____. Then all Fionna has to do is fling him _____ at her

NOUN   ADVERB

_____ enemy, and—poof!—no more evil _____!

ADJECTIVE   NOUN

From FIONNA AND CAKE MAD LIBS® • ™ & © Cartoon Network. (s13). Published in 2013 by
Price Stern Sloan, an imprint of Penguin Random House LLC, 345 Hudson Street, New York, NY 10014.

MAD LIBS® is fun to play with friends, but you can also play it by yourself! To begin with, DO NOT look at the story on the page below. Fill in the blanks on this page with the words called for. Then, using the words you have selected, fill in the blank spaces in the story.

Now you've created your own hilarious MAD LIBS® game!

PRINCE GUMBALL'S DIARY

ADJECTIVE _____

SILLY WORD _____

NOUN _____

PART OF THE BODY _____

NOUN _____

TYPE OF FOOD _____

NOUN _____

NOUN _____

TYPE OF LIQUID _____

PART OF THE BODY _____

ADJECTIVE _____

NOUN _____

PLURAL NOUN _____

PART OF THE BODY _____

PLURAL NOUN _____

NOUN _____

MAD LIBS
PRINCE GUMBALL'S DIARY

Dear Diary,

Oh, my _____ heart! One minute, Fionna blushes whenever I say
　　　　　ADJECTIVE

"_____," and the next, she couldn't care less about my princely
　SILLY WORD

_____. What is going on inside that fascinating _____ of
　NOUN　　　　　　　　　　　　　　　　　　　　　　　　　PART OF THE BODY

hers? First, when she rescued me from the Ice _____'s clutches, I
　　　　　　　　　　　　　　　　　　　　　　　　　　　　NOUN

asked her to go with me to the _____ Ball. She said yes. She was
　　　　　　　　　　　　　　　TYPE OF FOOD

totally diggin' my _____! But then, when the Ice _____
　　　　　　　　NOUN　　　　　　　　　　　　　　　　　　NOUN

put me in a prison of frozen _____ and, once again, Fionna saved my
　　　　　　　　　　　　TYPE OF LIQUID

_____, I asked her on a/an _____ date. You know
　PART OF THE BODY　　　　　　　　　ADJECTIVE

what she said? "No way, _____. Not interested. I think the reason I
　　　　　　　　　　NOUN

got all these guy _____ and no boyfriend is because I don't really
　　　　　　　PLURAL NOUN

wanna date any of 'em." I swear, my _____ burst into a million
　　　　　　　　　　　　　　　PART OF THE BODY

_____! Oh, diary. Maybe one day Fionna will be my one true
　PLURAL NOUN

_____!
　NOUN

MAD LIBS® is fun to play with friends, but you can also play it by yourself! To begin with, DO NOT look at the story on the page below. Fill in the blanks on this page with the words called for. Then, using the words you have selected, fill in the blank spaces in the story.

Now you've created your own hilarious MAD LIBS® game!

WHAT MIGHT HAVE BEEN, BY FIONNA

PERSON IN ROOM (MALE) _____

NOUN _____

PERSON IN ROOM _____

ADJECTIVE _____

PLURAL NOUN _____

A PLACE _____

PLURAL NOUN _____

PLURAL NOUN _____

NOUN _____

NOUN _____

NOUN _____

NOUN _____

PLURAL NOUN _____

Well, turns out my date with Prince _____ was actually a
                                                    PERSON IN ROOM (MALE)

date with the Ice _____ *disguised* as Prince Gumball. Gross.
                             NOUN

Then, by the time the *real* prince wanted to woo me, I told him no way,

_____. I'd had enough of dating for now. But still, I wondered—
PERSON IN ROOM

what might a real, _____ date with Gumball have been like? Would
                             ADJECTIVE

it have been romantic and full of rainbows and _____? Would we,
                                                               PLURAL NOUN

too, have raced to (the) _____ and sung a duet about our
                                       A PLACE

_____? Would we have told each other our deepest, darkest
  PLURAL NOUN

_____? I'm not sure, but at the end of the _____, I don't
  PLURAL NOUN   NOUN

need a/an _____ to make me happy. I know what kind of
                     NOUN

_____ I am, and I'll know who I want if and when the right
      NOUN

_____ comes along! Until then, it's just me and Cake, ruling the
      NOUN

roost as single _____!
                       PLURAL NOUN

From FIONNA AND CAKE MAD LIBS® • ™ & © Cartoon Network. (s13). Published in 2013 by
Price Stern Sloan, an imprint of Penguin Random House LLC, 345 Hudson Street, New York, NY 10014.

MAD LIBS® is fun to play with friends, but you can also play it by yourself! To begin with, DO NOT look at the story on the page below. Fill in the blanks on this page with the words called for. Then, using the words you have selected, fill in the blank spaces in the story.

Now you've created your own hilarious MAD LIBS® game!

THE ICE KING'S
OTHER FAN FICTION

NOUN _____

NOUN _____

ADJECTIVE _____

NOUN _____

PLURAL NOUN _____

NOUN _____

NOUN _____

ADVERB _____

SILLY WORD _____

NOUN _____

PART OF THE BODY _____

NOUN _____

NOUN _____

NOUN _____

ADJECTIVE _____

The Ice King was the _____ behind the tale of Fionna and Cake, but
NOUN

what other fan fiction has this _____ written? Here are a few of his
NOUN

_____ stories:
ADJECTIVE

- **The Ice King Goes to Hollywood:** The Ice King packs his

  _____ and heads to Hollywood in this classic rags-
  NOUN

  to-_____ tale, in which he lands a role in the movie *A/An*
  PLURAL NOUN

  _____ *Is Born*. His one speaking line is, "Have a nice
  NOUN

  _____!"
  NOUN

- **The Ice King's Day Off:** When Finn and Jake _____
  ADVERB

  disappear from the Land of _____, the Ice King finally gets
  SILLY WORD

  some peace and _____ to kidnap princesses whenever his
  NOUN

  little _____ pleases.
  PART OF THE BODY

- **The Ice King Gets Married:** In this heartfelt _____, the Ice
  NOUN

  King successfully captures Princess Bubble-_____ once and
  NOUN

  for all. The wedding scene is a real _____-jerker—mostly
  NOUN

  because no one wants the princess to marry the _____ king!
  ADJECTIVE

From FIONNA AND CAKE MAD LIBS® • ™ & © Cartoon Network. (s13). Published in 2013 by
Price Stern Sloan, an imprint of Penguin Random House LLC, 345 Hudson Street, New York, NY 10014.

REGULAR SHOW™

MAD LIBS®

PSS!

PRICE STERN SLOAN

An Imprint of Penguin Random House

INSTRUCTIONS

MAD LIBS® is a game for people who don't like games!
It can be played by one, two, three, four, or forty.

● RIDICULOUSLY SIMPLE DIRECTIONS

In this tablet you will find stories containing blank spaces where words are left out.
One player, the READER, selects one of these stories. The READER does not tell anyone
what the story is about. Instead, he/she asks the other players, the WRITERS, to give
him/her words. These words are used to fill in the blank spaces in the story.

● TO PLAY

The READER asks each WRITER in turn to call out a word—an adjective or a noun or
whatever the space calls for—and uses them to fill in the blank spaces in the story. The
result is a MAD LIBS® game.

When the READER then reads the completed MAD LIBS® game to the other players,
they will discover that they have written a story that is fantastic, screamingly funny,
shocking, silly, crazy, or just plain dumb—depending upon which words each WRITER
called out.

● EXAMPLE (*Before* and *After*)

"_____!" he said _____
                EXCLAMATION   ADVERB

as he jumped into his convertible _____ and
                                              NOUN

drove off with his _____ wife.
                        ADJECTIVE

"_____OUCH_____!" he said _____STUPIDLY_____
                EXCLAMATION   ADVERB

as he jumped into his convertible _____CAT_____ and
                                              NOUN

drove off with his _____BRAVE_____ wife.
                        ADJECTIVE

QUICK REVIEW

In case you have forgotten what adjectives, adverbs, nouns, and verbs are, here is a quick review:

An ADJECTIVE describes something or somebody. *Lumpy, soft, ugly, messy,* and *short* are adjectives.

An ADVERB tells how something is done. It modifies a verb and usually ends in "ly." *Modestly, stupidly, greedily,* and *carefully* are adverbs.

A NOUN is the name of a person, place, or thing. *Sidewalk, umbrella, bridle, bathtub,* and *nose* are nouns.

A VERB is an action word. *Run, pitch, jump,* and *swim* are verbs. Put the verbs in past tense if the directions say PAST TENSE. *Ran, pitched, jumped,* and *swam* are verbs in the past tense.

When we ask for A PLACE, we mean any sort of place: a country or city *(Spain, Cleveland)* or a room *(bathroom, kitchen).*

An EXCLAMATION or SILLY WORD is any sort of funny sound, gasp, grunt, or outcry, like *Wow!, Ouch!, Whomp!, Ick!,* and *Gadzooks!*

When we ask for specific words, like a NUMBER, a COLOR, an ANIMAL, or a PART OF THE BODY, we mean a word that is one of those things, like *seven, blue, horse,* or *head.*

When we ask for a PLURAL, it means more than one. For example, *cat* pluralized is *cats.*

MAD LIBS® is fun to play with friends, but you can also play it by yourself! To begin with, DO NOT look at the story on the page below. Fill in the blanks on this page with the words called for. Then, using the words you have selected, fill in the blank spaces in the story.

Now you've created your own hilarious MAD LIBS® game!

THE STORY OF MORDECAI AND RIGBY

NOUN _____

PLURAL NOUN _____

ADJECTIVE _____

NOUN _____

VERB ENDING IN "ING" _____

PERSON IN ROOM (MALE) _____

VERB _____

ADJECTIVE _____

ADVERB _____

PART OF THE BODY _____

ADJECTIVE _____

ADJECTIVE _____

ADVERB _____

PART OF THE BODY _____

PLURAL NOUN _____

VERB _____

Mordecai the blue _____ and Rigby the raccoon are

NOUN

not only the very best of _____, but they are also

PLURAL NOUN

_____ coworkers. They are employed as groundskeepers at a local

ADJECTIVE

_____, but they're much better at _____ off than doing

NOUN · VERB ENDING IN "ING"

any actual work. In fact, Mordecai and _____ would prefer to

PERSON IN ROOM (MALE)

do just about anything other than _____. Although these two

VERB

_____ friends are _____ inseparable, they don't always

ADJECTIVE · ADVERB

see _____ to eye. Mordecai is the more _____ of

PART OF THE BODY · ADJECTIVE

the two, but he still likes to have fun—usually _____

ADJECTIVE

fun. Rigby, on the other hand, is _____ immature, and he can be a

ADVERB

real pain in Mordecai's _____. But despite their differences,

PART OF THE BODY

these two _____ always manage to _____ and make up.

PLURAL NOUN · VERB

YEAH-YUH!

MAD LIBS® is fun to play with friends, but you can also play it by yourself! To begin with, DO NOT look at the story on the page below. Fill in the blanks on this page with the words called for. Then, using the words you have selected, fill in the blank spaces in the story.

Now you've created your own hilarious MAD LIBS® game!

A LOVE LETTER ABOUT SLACKING, BY RIGBY

ADJECTIVE _____

PART OF THE BODY (PLURAL) _____

ADJECTIVE _____

ADVERB _____

VERB ENDING IN "ING" _____

NOUN _____

PLURAL NOUN _____

EXCLAMATION _____

PLURAL NOUN _____

PART OF THE BODY _____

TYPE OF LIQUID _____

ADJECTIVE _____

PERSON IN ROOM (MALE) _____

VERB _____

ADJECTIVE _____

VERB _____

SILLY WORD _____

PLURAL NOUN _____

MAD LIBS®
A LOVE LETTER ABOUT
SLACKING, BY RIGBY

Dear Benson,

Mordecai and I do so love our jobs at the Park, but we love being _____
ADJECTIVE

even more. Although you are always on our _____ to get to
PART OF THE BODY (PLURAL)

work, we are _____ dudes and _____ do any work at all.
ADJECTIVE   ADVERB

You may think we're _____ the fountain, mowing the
VERB ENDING IN "ING"

_____, or replacing broken light _____, but—
NOUN   PLURAL NOUN

_____! Fooled you! We're probably playing video
EXCLAMATION

_____, listening to our favorite _____-banging
PLURAL NOUN   PART OF THE BODY

tunes, or hanging out at the _____. Shop. It takes a lot of skill to
TYPE OF LIQUID

be this _____ at slacking! _____and I should totally
ADJECTIVE   PERSON IN ROOM (MALE)

teach classes on how to _____. We'd be such _____
VERB   ADJECTIVE

teachers, am I right?! But wait, that means we'd actually have to _____.
VERB

_____—let's just keep _____ the way they are.
SILLY WORD   PLURAL NOUN

Stop talking!

Rigby

MAD LIBS® is fun to play with friends, but you can also play it by yourself! To begin with, DO NOT look at the story on the page below. Fill in the blanks on this page with the words called for. Then, using the words you have selected, fill in the blank spaces in the story.

Now you've created your own hilarious MAD LIBS® game!

VIDEO-GAME EXPERTS

ADJECTIVE _____

PLURAL NOUN _____

NUMBER _____

ADJECTIVE _____

VERB ENDING IN "ING" _____

NOUN _____

NOUN _____

ADJECTIVE _____

NOUN _____

ADJECTIVE _____

PLURAL NOUN _____

VERB ENDING IN "ING" _____

PART OF THE BODY _____

NOUN _____

SAME NOUN _____

PART OF THE BODY _____

MAD LIBS®
VIDEO-GAME EXPERTS

Mordecai: Dude, we are the most _____ video-game _____
                                   ADJECTIVE   PLURAL NOUN

ever, even though I am way better than you! I always get to be player one, and

you, loser, are always player _____.
                                NUMBER

Rigby: Yeah-yuh! We are so _____ at _____ *Dig Champs.*
                                 ADJECTIVE   VERB ENDING IN "ING"

The game _____ looks just like the cover, but the shovel and
            NOUN

_____ are pretty sucky.
      NOUN

Mordecai: And thanks to _____ old Benson, we never got to finish
                              ADJECTIVE

playing _____ *Choppers.* He made us stop to show us his
          NOUN

_____ House Rules.
   ADJECTIVE

Rigby: Hey, Benson, got any _____ by Joe Mama?
                                  PLURAL NOUN

Mordecai: And after _____ the Triple Thugs and beating the
                         VERB ENDING IN "ING"

Pink Guy by kicking him in the _____, we had to fight the
                                 PART OF THE BODY

_____, and no one beats the _____.
      NOUN   SAME NOUN

Rigby: Dude, do you know what our video-game awesomeness

deserves?

Mordecai and Rigby: _____ Pump!
                          PART OF THE BODY

MAD LIBS® is fun to play with friends, but you can also play it by yourself! To begin with, DO NOT look at the story on the page below. Fill in the blanks on this page with the words called for. Then, using the words you have selected, fill in the blank spaces in the story.

Now you've created your own hilarious MAD LIBS® game!

PUNCHIES

VERB _____

NOUN _____

VERB _____

NOUN _____

NOUN _____

ADJECTIVE _____

ADJECTIVE _____

NOUN _____

PART OF THE BODY _____

VERB ENDING IN "ING" _____

PART OF THE BODY _____

PLURAL NOUN _____

ADJECTIVE _____

NOUN _____

PERSON IN ROOM (MALE) _____

MAD LIBS
PUNCHIES

There's only one way to win an argument—Punchies!

Here are some rules:

1. It's always best to _____ your _____ unaware.
   <u>VERB</u>   <u>NOUN</u>

2. You don't have to _____ fair or give your
   <u>VERB</u>

   _____ any warning.
   <u>NOUN</u>

3. It doesn't matter if your _____ is smaller,
   <u>NOUN</u>

   _____ , or _____ .
   <u>ADJECTIVE</u>   <u>ADJECTIVE</u>

4. It's okay to hit your _____ anywhere, especially in
   <u>NOUN</u>

   the _____ .
   <u>PART OF THE BODY</u>

5. Try to yell "fist of pain" while _____ your
   <u>VERB ENDING IN "ING"</u>

   opponent.

6. If possible, put your opponent in a/an _____-
   <u>PART OF THE BODY</u>

   lock while giving _____ .
   <u>PLURAL NOUN</u>

7. The _____ version is Death Punchies, using the
   <u>ADJECTIVE</u>

   Death _____ of Death.
   <u>NOUN</u>

8. And the most important rule is that _____
   <u>PERSON IN ROOM (MALE)</u>

   always loses!

MAD LIBS® is fun to play with friends, but you can also play it by yourself! To begin with, DO NOT look at the story on the page below. Fill in the blanks on this page with the words called for. Then, using the words you have selected, fill in the blank spaces in the story.

Now you've created your own hilarious MAD LIBS® game!

ROCK-PAPER-SCISSORS

VERB _____

NOUN _____

NOUN _____

NOUN _____

NOUN _____

ADJECTIVE _____

NOUN _____

PERSON IN ROOM (MALE) _____

SAME PERSON IN ROOM (MALE) _____

NOUN _____

NOUN _____

ADJECTIVE _____

NOUN _____

NOUN _____

NUMBER _____

ADJECTIVE _____

NOUN _____

NOUN _____

If Punchies can't _____ an argument, whether it's about who gets to
VERB

drive the golf _____ or who has to ask Muscle Man for his
NOUN

_____, the next best thing is rock-paper-_____! Pops
NOUN   NOUN

claims that back in Lolliland they played it, too, but they called it

quartz-_____-shears. And Benson says that it's a/an _____
NOUN   ADJECTIVE

game, and it's actually against the _____ Rules. Somehow Rigby
NOUN

always seems to beat _____, but _____
PERSON IN ROOM (MALE)   SAME PERSON IN ROOM (MALE)

eventually ended Rigby's winning _____ when a bunch of
NOUN

_____ ducks showed up. And during one _____ battle of
NOUN   ADJECTIVE

rock-_____-scissors, Mordecai and Rigby played the
NOUN

_____ over _____ times and it caused a totally
NOUN   NUMBER

_____ event. A green _____ appeared and almost caused
ADJECTIVE   NOUN

the end of the _____. OOOOOH!
NOUN

MAD LIBS® is fun to play with friends, but you can also play it by yourself! To begin with, DO NOT look at the story on the page below. Fill in the blanks on this page with the words called for. Then, using the words you have selected, fill in the blank spaces in the story.

Now you've created your own hilarious MAD LIBS® game!

THIS IS OUR JAM!
MORDECAI AND THE RIGBYS

NOUN _____

PART OF THE BODY _____

NOUN _____

PART OF THE BODY (PLURAL) _____

NUMBER _____

PART OF THE BODY (PLURAL) _____

VERB _____

NOUN _____

ADJECTIVE _____

ADJECTIVE _____

VERB _____

SAME VERB _____

NOUN _____

NOUN _____

NOUN _____

ADJECTIVE _____

VERB _____

SAME VERB _____

Dudes! The most excellent _____ in the world is Mordecai and the

NOUN

Rigbys. And our best _____-banging tune is "Party Time." So

PART OF THE BODY

grab your electric _____ and join our jam!

NOUN

Your eyes staring into my _____.

PART OF THE BODY (PLURAL)

Who am I but a guy with _____ eyes on the prize.

NUMBER

And the prize in my _____ is ten times

PART OF THE BODY (PLURAL)

The prize in your eyes as I _____ you good night.

VERB

Your _____ is the fire that rocks my soul,

NOUN

Gonna remember it until I grow _____,

ADJECTIVE

'Cause life is too _____, we gotta do things right.

ADJECTIVE

So, baby, let's just _____ tonight.

VERB

Baby, let's just _____ tonight.

SAME VERB

We've come out on top, we're in front of the _____,

NOUN

We're here to rock out and have a good _____,

NOUN

'Cause the past is the _____ and the future is _____.

NOUN   ADJECTIVE

So, baby, let's just _____ tonight.

VERB

Baby, let's just _____ tonight.

SAME VERB

MAD LIBS® is fun to play with friends, but you can also play it by yourself! To begin with, DO NOT look at the story on the page below. Fill in the blanks on this page with the words called for. Then, using the words you have selected, fill in the blank spaces in the story.

Now you've created your own hilarious MAD LIBS® game!

GET BACK TO WORK!, BY BENSON

NOUN _____

ADVERB _____

NOUN _____

ADJECTIVE _____

PLURAL NOUN _____

VERB ENDING IN "ING" _____

NOUN _____

ADJECTIVE _____

TYPE OF FOOD (PLURAL) _____

ADJECTIVE _____

NOUN _____

SAME NOUN _____

VERB _____

PLURAL NOUN _____

ADJECTIVE _____

Benson here. I am the _____ of Mordecai and Rigby, and I
_____NOUN_____

_____ have to tell them to get back to work! They are the worst
_____ADVERB_____

_____-keepers and are completely _____ at everything
_____NOUN_____   _____ADJECTIVE_____

they do, whether it's setting up _____, _____ out
                                  ____PLURAL NOUN____ __VERB ENDING IN "ING"__

the fountain, or serving customers at the Snack _____. Those
                                                 _____NOUN_____

_____, no-good slackers drive me _____! They
____ADJECTIVE____   __TYPE OF FOOD (PLURAL)__

never, ever listen to me. If they did, they'd see that I've been trying to teach

them some _____ responsibility and to take pride in a/an
           _____ADJECTIVE_____

_____ well done. But they wouldn't know a/an _____
_____NOUN_____   ____SAME NOUN____

well done if they paid someone to do it for them! And even then, they'd probably

_____ it up, considering they can't even follow the simplest of
_____VERB_____

_____! They're more worried about looking _____ than
___PLURAL NOUN___   _____ADJECTIVE_____

doing their job!

MAD LIBS® is fun to play with friends, but you can also play it by yourself! To begin with, DO NOT look at the story on the page below. Fill in the blanks on this page with the words called for. Then, using the words you have selected, fill in the blank spaces in the story.

Now you've created your own hilarious MAD LIBS® game!

I KNOW EVERYTHING, BY SKIPS

ADJECTIVE _____

ADVERB _____

PLURAL NOUN _____

ADJECTIVE _____

NOUN _____

PERSON IN ROOM (MALE) _____

ADJECTIVE _____

ADJECTIVE _____

ADJECTIVE _____

PERSON IN ROOM (MALE) _____

NOUN _____

NOUN _____

ADJECTIVE _____

VERB _____

PART OF THE BODY (PLURAL) _____

Mordecai and Rigby sure are _____ to have me around! That's
_____ADJECTIVE

because I _____ come to their rescue. Benson threatens to fire those
_____ADVERB

two _____ all the time, but due to my _____ yeti nature
_____PLURAL NOUN_____ADJECTIVE

and the _____ that comes from immortality, I'm able to convince
_____NOUN

Benson to let them keep their jobs. Mordecai and _____
_____PERSON IN ROOM (MALE)

usually argue with me about how to get them out of these _____
_____ADJECTIVE

situations. They need to listen to my _____ motto: We tried it
_____ADJECTIVE

the _____ way, now we do it the _____ way! Yes,
_____ADJECTIVE_____PERSON IN ROOM (MALE)

that skinny blue _____ and striped-tail _____ will
_____NOUN_____NOUN

always drive me _____, but I just can't _____ myself—
_____ADJECTIVE_____VERB

I'll always be there to save their _____.
_____PART OF THE BODY (PLURAL)

From REGULAR SHOW MAD LIBS® • ™ & © Cartoon Network. (s13). Published in 2013 by Price Stern Sloan,
an imprint of Penguin Random House LLC, 345 Hudson Street, New York, NY 10014.

MAD LIBS® is fun to play with friends, but you can also play it by yourself! To begin with, DO NOT look at the story on the page below. Fill in the blanks on this page with the words called for. Then, using the words you have selected, fill in the blank spaces in the story.

Now you've created your own hilarious MAD LIBS® game!

BENSON'S HOUSE RULES, BY MORDECAI AND RIGBY

PERSON IN ROOM (MALE) _____

NOUN _____

ADJECTIVE _____

PLURAL NOUN _____

NOUN _____

NOUN _____

PART OF THE BODY (PLURAL) _____

NOUN _____

PLURAL NOUN _____

EXCLAMATION _____

ADJECTIVE _____

PLURAL NOUN _____

PLURAL NOUN _____

PLURAL NOUN _____

MAD LIBS®
BENSON'S HOUSE RULES,
BY MORDECAI AND RIGBY

Hey, _____, you gotta chillax, dude. Your book of
     PERSON IN ROOM (MALE)

_____ Rules is, like, totally _____. How do you expect
    NOUN   ADJECTIVE

anyone to live by _____ like these?
            PLURAL NOUN

- No _____-playing after 10 p.m.
    NOUN

- No rock-paper-_____
          NOUN

- No _____ on the table
    PART OF THE BODY (PLURAL)

- No food on the _____
          NOUN

- No _____ on the floor
    PLURAL NOUN

- No Punchies—_____!
      EXCLAMATION

- No _____ camping
    ADJECTIVE

- No prank _____
     PLURAL NOUN

- No oversize novelty _____ on work time
         PLURAL NOUN

- No video _____ . . . NOOOOOOOO!
    PLURAL NOUN

MAD LIBS® is fun to play with friends, but you can also play it by yourself! To begin with, DO NOT look at the story on the page below. Fill in the blanks on this page with the words called for. Then, using the words you have selected, fill in the blank spaces in the story.

Now you've created your own hilarious MAD LIBS® game!

LIFE IS EVER SO JOLLY!, BY POPS

ADJECTIVE _____

VERB _____

PLURAL NOUN _____

ADJECTIVE _____

NOUN _____

PERSON IN ROOM (MALE) _____

NOUN _____

PLURAL NOUN _____

ANIMAL (PLURAL) _____

PLURAL NOUN _____

VERB ENDING IN "ING" _____

NOUN _____

NOUN _____

VERB _____

NOUN _____

ADJECTIVE _____

MAD LIBS
LIFE IS EVER SO JOLLY!, BY POPS

Oh, I do love Mordecai and Rigby, even though they are ever so _____!
ADJECTIVE

They are such rascals and they _____ Benson crazy, but since I'm
VERB

Benson's boss, I let those silly _____ stay. My _____ old
PLURAL NOUN   ADJECTIVE

dad owns the Park, but I don't do a/an _____ of work there. Oh no,
NOUN

I let _____ worry his _____-filled head about all
PERSON IN ROOM (MALE)   NOUN

that. I like spending my days trying to catch _____ in a jar, wrestling
PLURAL NOUN

polar _____, baking _____, or _____
ANIMAL (PLURAL)   PLURAL NOUN   VERB ENDING IN "ING"

poems. And I am the most fancy _____ you will ever see. I've even
NOUN

written a/an _____ about fanciness: *Fanciness: Theory and Practical*
NOUN

Application. I do hope you will _____ it. Anyone for a game of
VERB

quartz-_____-shears? Good show, _____ good show!
NOUN   ADJECTIVE

From REGULAR SHOW MAD LIBS® • ™ & © Cartoon Network. (s13). Published in 2013 by Price Stern Sloan, an imprint of Penguin Random House LLC, 345 Hudson Street, New York, NY 10014.

MAD LIBS® is fun to play with friends, but you can also play it by yourself! To begin with, DO NOT look at the story on the page below. Fill in the blanks on this page with the words called for. Then, using the words you have selected, fill in the blank spaces in the story.

Now you've created your own hilarious MAD LIBS® game!

LOVE SONG TO MARGARET, BY MORDECAI

ADJECTIVE _____

NOUN _____

VERB ENDING IN "ING" _____

ADJECTIVE _____

VERB ENDING IN "ING" _____

NOUN _____

ADJECTIVE _____

PLURAL NOUN _____

PART OF THE BODY _____

ADJECTIVE _____

PLURAL NOUN _____

PART OF THE BODY (PLURAL) _____

VERB ENDING IN "ING" _____

NOUN _____

ADJECTIVE _____

MAD LIBS®
LOVE SONG TO MARGARET, BY MORDECAI

I have the most _____ crush on Margaret. I even wrote a sweet
                        ADJECTIVE

_____ for her that goes something like this:
     NOUN

Doo-doo-doo-doo-doo!

_____ with Margaret just-a feels too _____, like I
VERB ENDING IN "ING"   ADJECTIVE

knew it would.

_____ together and a-having a/an _____ , and I
VERB ENDING IN "ING"   NOUN

hope it lasts forever!

I can't believe how _____ she is; my insides feel like knotted
                      ADJECTIVE

_____ .
  PLURAL NOUN

Her pretty _____ and those _____ long legs.
           PART OF THE BODY   ADJECTIVE

And I hope someday we are more than just _____!
                                          PLURAL NOUN

Do you remember last night when our _____ touched?
                                    PART OF THE BODY (PLURAL)

We were _____ for the dice, and you were laughing and
        VERB ENDING IN "ING"

such . . .

Take one roll, and then take a/an _____ on me.
                                  NOUN

And then maybe you'll see.

How _____ we can be.
    ADJECTIVE

From REGULAR SHOW MAD LIBS® • ™ & © Cartoon Network. (s13). Published in 2013 by Price Stern Sloan, an imprint of Penguin Random House LLC, 345 Hudson Street, New York, NY 10014.

MAD LIBS® is fun to play with friends, but you can also play it by yourself! To begin with, DO NOT look at the story on the page below. Fill in the blanks on this page with the words called for. Then, using the words you have selected, fill in the blank spaces in the story.

Now you've created your own hilarious MAD LIBS® game!

MUCHO MACHO, BY MUSCLE MAN

PART OF THE BODY _____

NOUN _____

ADJECTIVE _____

NOUN _____

NOUN _____

COLOR _____

ADJECTIVE _____

PLURAL NOUN _____

ADJECTIVE _____

ANIMAL _____

ADJECTIVE _____

PLURAL NOUN _____

ADVERB _____

NOUN _____

ADJECTIVE _____

NOUN _____

NUMBER _____

PART OF THE BODY (PLURAL) _____

MAD LIBS®
MUCHO MACHO,
BY MUSCLE MAN

Hey, Mordecai and Rigby—in your _____! I am the one and
                                             PART OF THE BODY

only Muscle Man, and I will wipe the _____ with you! You are a/an
                                         NOUN

_____ blue jay and a pipsqueak _____, while I am the
ADJECTIVE   NOUN

world's most attractive green _____, with stylin' _____ hair,
                            NOUN   COLOR

a/an _____ body, and large _____ . With my _____
      ADJECTIVE   PLURAL NOUN   ADJECTIVE

fashion sense, I should be strutting on a/an _____-walk! I'm sure
                                       ANIMAL

you are jealous of my _____ T-shirt, my tight _____,
                       ADJECTIVE   PLURAL NOUN

and my _____ sexy shoes. And don't forget about my rockin'
             ADVERB

girlfriend, Starla Gutsmandottir. She is the _____ of my life, and
                                    NOUN

I'm sure the two of you are super jealous of our relationship. We are

_____! And you two losers are the worst _____-keepers
ADJECTIVE   NOUN

ever. Hi _____ Ghost and I could whup your
                 NUMBER

_____ any day of the week. You know who can't even help
PART OF THE BODY (PLURAL)

you? MY MOM!

MAD LIBS® is fun to play with friends, but you can also play it by yourself! To begin with, DO NOT look at the story on the page below. Fill in the blanks on this page with the words called for. Then, using the words you have selected, fill in the blank spaces in the story.

Now you've created your own hilarious MAD LIBS® game!

PRANKSTERS PAR EXCELLENCE

VERB ENDING IN "ING" _____

PERSON IN ROOM (MALE) _____

ADJECTIVE _____

NUMBER _____

SAME PERSON IN ROOM (MALE) _____

NOUN _____

PART OF THE BODY (PLURAL) _____

ADJECTIVE _____

ADJECTIVE _____

ADJECTIVE _____

NOUN _____

ADVERB _____

ADJECTIVE _____

PERSON IN ROOM _____

PLURAL NOUN _____

PART OF THE BODY _____

MAD LIBS®
PRANKSTERS PAR EXCELLENCE

Although Mordecai and Rigby hate _____, they love pranking.
<u>VERB ENDING IN "ING"</u>

They once pranked _____ by giving him a/an _____
<u>PERSON IN ROOM (MALE)</u> <u>ADJECTIVE</u>

lottery ticket worth _____ dollars. But since _____
<u>NUMBER</u> <u>SAME PERSON IN ROOM (MALE)</u>

believes that "one good _____ deserves another," Mordecai and
<u>NOUN</u>

Rigby better watch their _____! Mordecai and Rigby's most
<u>PART OF THE BODY (PLURAL)</u>

_____ prank was almost the demise of their _____
<u>ADJECTIVE</u> <u>ADJECTIVE</u>

friendship. The _____ slackers learned how to make prank calls by
<u>ADJECTIVE</u>

watching a funny Internet _____ called "Master Prank Caller."
<u>NOUN</u>

Mordecai and Rigby decided to _____ prank the Master Prank
<u>ADVERB</u>

Caller himself, which landed them in a totally _____ duel with their
<u>ADJECTIVE</u>

prankster idol. Fortunately, Skips, _____, and Pops rescued
<u>PERSON IN ROOM</u>

Mordecai and Rigby. Will those two _____ ever learn? No!
<u>PLURAL NOUN</u>

_____ Pump!
<u>PART OF THE BODY</u>

MAD LIBS® is fun to play with friends, but you can also play it by yourself! To begin with, DO NOT look at the story on the page below. Fill in the blanks on this page with the words called for. Then, using the words you have selected, fill in the blank spaces in the story.

Now you've created your own hilarious MAD LIBS® game!

A LOVE LETTER FROM EILEEN TO RIGBY

NOUN _____

ADJECTIVE _____

ADJECTIVE _____

VERB _____

ADJECTIVE _____

PART OF THE BODY _____

VERB _____

VERB ENDING IN "ING" _____

NOUN _____

ADVERB _____

PLURAL NOUN _____

NOUN _____

ADJECTIVE _____

NOUN _____

ADJECTIVE _____

COLOR _____

ADJECTIVE _____

NOUN _____

To my dearest Rigby,

I may just be a/an _____ with glasses and you are a/an _____
           NOUN   ADJECTIVE

raccoon, but I know that we could make a/an _____ couple if you
                                        ADJECTIVE

would just _____ me. I was so _____ that time that we
              VERB   ADJECTIVE

went to the movies and I put my _____ in your bowl of popcorn.
                                  PART OF THE BODY

All I wanted was for you to _____ me! And that time we went
                              VERB

_____—I think you finally realized that you really do like me
VERB ENDING IN "ING"

because you threw a/an _____ of hot dogs at me! The night ended
                        NOUN

_____ when we played video _____ sitting on the
     ADVERB   PLURAL NOUN

_____. That's _____ love in my _____! I just
   NOUN   ADJECTIVE   NOUN

know that my _____ ponytail and little _____ tail could
            ADJECTIVE   COLOR

make you _____ for the rest of your _____.
          ADJECTIVE   NOUN

Love,

Eileen

From REGULAR SHOW MAD LIBS® • ™ & © Cartoon Network. (s13). Published in 2013 by Price Stern Sloan,
an imprint of Penguin Random House LLC, 345 Hudson Street, New York, NY 10014.

MAD LIBS® is fun to play with friends, but you can also play it by yourself! To begin with, DO NOT look at the story on the page below. Fill in the blanks on this page with the words called for. Then, using the words you have selected, fill in the blank spaces in the story.

Now you've created your own hilarious MAD LIBS® game!

"IT'S ANYTHING BUT . . ."

ADJECTIVE _____

NOUN _____

ADJECTIVE _____

NOUN _____

EXCLAMATION _____

NOUN _____

PLURAL NOUN _____

TYPE OF LIQUID _____

NUMBER _____

ADJECTIVE _____

ADJECTIVE _____

NOUN _____

VERB ENDING IN "ING" _____

PLURAL NOUN _____

ADJECTIVE _____

ADJECTIVE _____

NOUN _____

ADJECTIVE _____

MAD LIBS

"IT'S ANYTHING BUT . . ."

Home, _____ home. Mordecai and Rigby live in a/an
           ADJECTIVE

_____ in the Park. They share the space with Pops, but they have to
     NOUN

be careful, because they don't want to see Pops _____ after he's just
                                                    ADJECTIVE

come out of the _____. _____! Mordecai and Rigby
                     NOUN   EXCLAMATION

spend most of their time chillin' on the _____ playing video games
                                               NOUN

or hangin' in the kitchen eating blueberry _____ and drinking
                                                PLURAL NOUN

gallons of _____. Muscle Man and Hi _____ Ghost live
              TYPE OF LIQUID   NUMBER

in a/an _____ trailer. It's kind of a/an _____ dump
             ADJECTIVE   ADJECTIVE

because they never clean it. OOOOOOH! Skips's house doubles as the golf-

_____ garage. When he's not _____ golf carts, he's
     NOUN   VERB ENDING IN "ING"

lifting _____. Benson lives in a/an _____ apartment,
           PLURAL NOUN   ADJECTIVE

and his _____ neighbor across the hall has a serious _____ on
            ADJECTIVE   NOUN

him.

Be it ever so _____, there's no place like home.
                  ADJECTIVE

From REGULAR SHOW MAD LIBS® • ™ & © Cartoon Network. (s13). Published in 2013 by Price Stern Sloan,
an imprint of Penguin Random House LLC, 345 Hudson Street, New York, NY 10014.

MAD LIBS® is fun to play with friends, but you can also play it by yourself! To begin with, DO NOT look at the story on the page below. Fill in the blanks on this page with the words called for. Then, using the words you have selected, fill in the blank spaces in the story.

Now you've created your own hilarious MAD LIBS® game!

A BUNCH OF BABY DUCKS, BY MORDECAI AND RIGBY

NOUN_____

PLURAL NOUN_____

EXCLAMATION_____

PLURAL NOUN_____

VERB (PAST TENSE)_____

VERB_____

ADJECTIVE_____

NOUN_____

ADJECTIVE_____

ADJECTIVE_____

NOUN_____

NOUN_____

NOUN_____

ADJECTIVE_____

MAD LIBS®
A BUNCH OF BABY DUCKS,
BY MORDECAI AND RIGBY

Rigby: Dude, remember that time when we were cleaning out the

_____, and we found that bunch of baby _____?

NOUN   PLURAL NOUN

Mordecai: _____, dude! Remember how those baby _____

EXCLAMATION   PLURAL NOUN

thought you were their mom?

Rigby: Yeah, that sucked. They even _____ around in my cereal

VERB (PAST TENSE)

bowl. And they didn't listen when I told them to _____ off.

VERB

Mordecai: True, but they were _____ learners. They beat

ADJECTIVE

you playing _____ games and did some pretty

NOUN

_____ karate chops.

ADJECTIVE

Rigby: Dude, those _____ ducks were more like thugs.

ADJECTIVE

Mordecai: Yeah, I guess so, but then we had to save them when that

creepy _____ kidnapped them.

NOUN

Rigby: Lucky their _____ showed up and flew us there!

NOUN

Mordecai: Mmm-hmm. But they didn't really need our help, since

they turned into a giant _____ and nuked that guy.

NOUN

Rigby: Yeah, that was so _____. I kind of wish I could have

ADJECTIVE

been their mom.

From REGULAR SHOW MAD LIBS® • ™ & © Cartoon Network. (s13). Published in 2013 by Price Stern Sloan, an imprint of Penguin Random House LLC, 345 Hudson Street, New York, NY 10014.

MAD LIBS® is fun to play with friends, but you can also play it by yourself! To begin with, DO NOT look at the story on the page below. Fill in the blanks on this page with the words called for. Then, using the words you have selected, fill in the blank spaces in the story.

Now you've created your own hilarious MAD LIBS® game!

ONE-CHEEK WONDER

NOUN _____

ADJECTIVE _____

PART OF THE BODY _____

PERSON IN ROOM _____

NOUN _____

NOUN _____

ADJECTIVE _____

NOUN _____

ADJECTIVE _____

NUMBER _____

NUMBER _____

ADJECTIVE _____

MAD LIBS®
ONE-CHEEK WONDER

It's a little-known _____ that Rigby had a/an _____ accident
NOUN   ADJECTIVE

that cost him one of his _____ cheeks! So what happened?
PART OF THE BODY

Everyone knows that Rigby always loses at Punchies—even _____
PERSON IN ROOM

beat him. So he should have thought better than to challenge Skips to a/an

_____ of Punchies. At the end of the match, Rigby had to be rushed
NOUN

off to the emergency _____ to have _____ surgery on his
NOUN   ADJECTIVE

left butt cheek. The surgeon must have flunked out of _____ school,
NOUN

because Rigby now has a/an _____ scar on his butt, and it makes
ADJECTIVE

him look like he has _____ cheeks! Try not to talk about this in
NUMBER

front of Rigby or call him the _____-cheek wonder, because he's
NUMBER

really _____ about it. Poor Rigby, with cheeks like that, he'll never
ADJECTIVE

be able to play Punchies again . . .

From REGULAR SHOW MAD LIBS® • ™ & © Cartoon Network. (s13). Published in 2013 by Price Stern Sloan,
an imprint of Penguin Random House LLC, 345 Hudson Street, New York, NY 10014.

MAD LIBS® is fun to play with friends, but you can also play it by yourself! To begin with, DO NOT look at the story on the page below. Fill in the blanks on this page with the words called for. Then, using the words you have selected, fill in the blank spaces in the story.

Now you've created your own hilarious MAD LIBS® game!

OUR FAVORITE FOODS, BY MORDECAI AND RIGBY

NOUN _____

NOUN _____

NOUN _____

VERB _____

ADJECTIVE _____

ADJECTIVE _____

NOUN _____

TYPE OF LIQUID _____

PERSON IN ROOM (MALE) _____

PLURAL NOUN _____

NUMBER _____

ANIMAL (PLURAL) _____

PLURAL NOUN _____

TYPE OF LIQUID _____

VERB _____

MAD LIBS®
OUR FAVORITE FOODS,
BY MORDECAI AND RIGBY

Whether we're sitting on the _____ playing _____ games or
NOUN   NOUN

just chilling in the _____, we love to eat and _____!
NOUN   VERB

Here are some of our _____ foods:
ADJECTIVE

• _____ doughnuts from the Snack Bar
ADJECTIVE

• Grilled _____ deluxe sandwiches (that we steal from Benson)
NOUN

• Gallons of _____, dude!
TYPE OF LIQUID

• Pizza, because _____ is the Pizza King!
PERSON IN ROOM (MALE)

• Soggy Oat _____—best cereal ever!
PLURAL NOUN

• The Ulti-Meatum—but remember, only _____ per guest
NUMBER

• Super Extra Premium Hot _____—perfect for any BBQ
ANIMAL (PLURAL)

• Delicious _____ from Taco'Clock
PLURAL NOUN

• Rig-_____—which makes us more smarter
TYPE OF LIQUID

• But we will never have another Mississippi Queen because it will

_____ us up!
VERB

MAD LIBS® is fun to play with friends, but you can also play it by yourself! To begin with, DO NOT look at the story on the page below. Fill in the blanks on this page with the words called for. Then, using the words you have selected, fill in the blank spaces in the story.

Now you've created your own hilarious MAD LIBS® game!

GREEN LOVIN'

ADJECTIVE _____

PERSON IN ROOM (MALE) _____

PART OF THE BODY _____

ADJECTIVE _____

PART OF THE BODY _____

VERB ENDING IN "ING" _____

ADJECTIVE _____

ADJECTIVE _____

VERB (PAST TENSE) _____

VERB ENDING IN "ING" _____

ADJECTIVE _____

ADJECTIVE _____

PART OF THE BODY _____

ADJECTIVE _____

PART OF THE BODY (PLURAL) _____

NOUN _____

MAD LIBS®
GREEN LOVIN'

Muscle Man and Starla are a/an _____ green match made in heaven.
                                    ADJECTIVE

But it wasn't always that way. Muscle Man, whose real name is

_____, had his _____ broken when Starla
PERSON IN ROOM (MALE)   PART OF THE BODY

dumped him. Muscle Man was a/an _____ mess. He stuffed his
                                         ADJECTIVE

_____ hole with Muscle Maker 3000 and sat in his shower
PART OF THE BODY

_____. But Mordecai and Rigby came up with a/an
VERB ENDING IN "ING"

_____ plan to get the _____ couple back together. They
   ADJECTIVE   ADJECTIVE

figured that if Mordecai _____ Starla and then broke up with her,
                          VERB (PAST TENSE)

she'd go _____ back to Muscle Man. But their plan was totally
          VERB ENDING IN "ING"

_____—when Mordecai dumped Starla, she went on a/an
   ADJECTIVE

_____ rampage and destroyed the Park. Luckily, Muscle Man came
   ADJECTIVE

to the rescue. He finally spoke to Starla from his _____ and
                                                     PART OF THE BODY

told her his _____ feelings for her. Then Muscle Man picked up
              ADJECTIVE

Starla up with his _____, and they walked off into the
                    PART OF THE BODY (PLURAL)

_____—greenly ever after.
   NOUN

MAD LIBS® is fun to play with friends, but you can also play it by yourself! To begin with, DO NOT look at the story on the page below. Fill in the blanks on this page with the words called for. Then, using the words you have selected, fill in the blank spaces in the story.

Now you've created your own hilarious MAD LIBS® game!

DEATH KWON DO!

ADJECTIVE _____

VERB ENDING IN "ING" _____

PLURAL NOUN_____

VERB _____

NOUN _____

PART OF THE BODY (PLURAL) _____

NOUN _____

ADJECTIVE _____

ADVERB _____

PLURAL NOUN _____

ADJECTIVE _____

PART OF THE BODY _____

PLURAL NOUN _____

ADJECTIVE _____

NOUN _____

ADJECTIVE _____

NOUN _____

MAD LIBS®
DEATH KWON DO!

Dude, if you're like Rigby and you're sick and _____ of
_____ at Punchies all the time, get yourself down to the Death

ADJECTIVE

VERB ENDING IN "ING"

Kwon Do Studio. There you can learn kicks, chops, and _____,

PLURAL NOUN

and _____ your full potential today! Discover how to do the Bicep

VERB

_____ of Death, _____ Lifts of Death, the Pelvic

NOUN   PART OF THE BODY (PLURAL)

_____ of Death, and the most _____ move of them

NOUN   ADJECTIVE

all—the Death Punch of Death. But be sure to use this special move

_____, as it can create total _____ and destruction.

ADVERB   PLURAL NOUN

And to make your _____ moves even more kick-

ADJECTIVE

_____, get yourself a pair of cutoff jean _____ and

PART OF THE BODY   PLURAL NOUN

a/an _____ mullet hair-_____. This, my kwon do friend,

ADJECTIVE   NOUN

will transform you from a/an _____ loser into a master of the

ADJECTIVE

_____!

NOUN

From REGULAR SHOW MAD LIBS® • ™ & © Cartoon Network. (s13). Published in 2013 by Price Stern Sloan, an imprint of Penguin Random House LLC, 345 Hudson Street, New York, NY 10014.

MAD LIBS® is fun to play with friends, but you can also play it by yourself! To begin with, DO NOT look at the story on the page below. Fill in the blanks on this page with the words called for. Then, using the words you have selected, fill in the blank spaces in the story.

Now you've created your own hilarious MAD LIBS® game!

DUDE, YOU KNOW WHAT YOU SHOULD DO . . . ?

ADJECTIVE _____

PERSON IN ROOM (MALE) _____

VERB _____

ADJECTIVE _____

VERB _____

PLURAL NOUN _____

NOUN _____

PLURAL NOUN _____

ADJECTIVE _____

ADJECTIVE _____

ADJECTIVE _____

PLURAL NOUN _____

ADJECTIVE _____

ADJECTIVE _____

MAD LIBS®
DUDE, YOU KNOW WHAT YOU SHOULD DO . . . ?

Oooooh, Mordecai, if you want to be a totally _____ dude, like
ADJECTIVE

_____, you need to _____ a hit song. You'll become
PERSON IN ROOM (MALE)   VERB

rich and _____, so you won't have to _____ anymore
ADJECTIVE   VERB

and _____ will go crazy for you! Hurry up and grab your electric
PLURAL NOUN

_____, strum some _____, and write some
NOUN   PLURAL NOUN

_____ lyrics! Actually, that doesn't sound very _____.
ADJECTIVE   ADJECTIVE

Maybe this isn't as _____ as we thought it would be. Or maybe you
ADJECTIVE

just don't have the _____ and are just a/an _____ loser.
PLURAL NOUN   ADJECTIVE

But there might still be some hope for you. Maybe you could write a/an

_____ ringtone. How hard could that be? Mmm-hmm.
ADJECTIVE

From REGULAR SHOW MAD LIBS® • ™ & © Cartoon Network. (s13). Published in 2013 by Price Stern Sloan, an imprint of Penguin Random House LLC, 345 Hudson Street, New York, NY 10014.

UNCLE GRANDPA

MAD·LIBS

PSS!

PRICE STERN SLOAN

An Imprint of Penguin Random House

INSTRUCTIONS

MAD LIBS® is a game for people who don't like games!
It can be played by one, two, three, four, or forty.

• RIDICULOUSLY SIMPLE DIRECTIONS

In this tablet you will find stories containing blank spaces where words are left out.
One player, the READER, selects one of these stories. The READER does not tell anyone
what the story is about. Instead, he/she asks the other players, the WRITERS, to give
him/her words. These words are used to fill in the blank spaces in the story.

• TO PLAY

The READER asks each WRITER in turn to call out a word—an adjective or a noun or
whatever the space calls for—and uses them to fill in the blank spaces in the story. The
result is a MAD LIBS® game.

When the READER then reads the completed MAD LIBS® game to the other players,
they will discover that they have written a story that is fantastic, screamingly funny,
shocking, silly, crazy, or just plain dumb—depending upon which words each WRITER
called out.

• EXAMPLE (*Before* and *After*)

"_____!" he said _____
          EXCLAMATION   ADVERB

as he jumped into his convertible _____ and
                                          NOUN

drove off with his _____ wife.
                        ADJECTIVE

"_____OUCH_____!" he said _____STUPIDLY_____
          EXCLAMATION   ADVERB

as he jumped into his convertible _____CAT_____ and
                                          NOUN

drove off with his _____BRAVE_____ wife.
                        ADJECTIVE

QUICK REVIEW

In case you have forgotten what adjectives, adverbs, nouns, and verbs are, here is a quick review:

An ADJECTIVE describes something or somebody. *Lumpy, soft, ugly, messy,* and *short* are adjectives.

An ADVERB tells how something is done. It modifies a verb and usually ends in "ly." *Modestly, stupidly, greedily,* and *carefully* are adverbs.

A NOUN is the name of a person, place, or thing. *Sidewalk, umbrella, bridle, bathtub,* and *nose* are nouns.

A VERB is an action word. *Run, pitch, jump,* and *swim* are verbs. Put the verbs in past tense if the directions say PAST TENSE. *Ran, pitched, jumped,* and *swam* are verbs in the past tense.

When we ask for A PLACE, we mean any sort of place: a country or city *(Spain, Cleveland)* or a room *(bathroom, kitchen).*

An EXCLAMATION or SILLY WORD is any sort of funny sound, gasp, grunt, or outcry, like *Wow!, Ouch!, Whomp!, Ick!,* and *Gadzooks!*

When we ask for specific words, like a NUMBER, a COLOR, an ANIMAL, or a PART OF THE BODY, we mean a word that is one of those things, like *seven, blue, horse,* or *head.*

When we ask for a PLURAL, it means more than one. For example, *cat* pluralized is *cats.*

MAD LIBS® is fun to play with friends, but you can also play it by yourself! To begin with, DO NOT look at the story on the page below. Fill in the blanks on this page with the words called for. Then, using the words you have selected, fill in the blank spaces in the story.

Now you've created your own hilarious MAD LIBS® game!

EMBRACE THE WEIRD

NOUN _____

ADJECTIVE _____

A PLACE _____

NOUN _____

ADJECTIVE _____

NOUN _____

ADVERB _____

PART OF THE BODY _____

PERSON IN ROOM (MALE) _____

ADJECTIVE _____

PLURAL NOUN _____

NOUN _____

ANIMAL _____

NOUN _____

ADJECTIVE _____

NOUN _____

ADJECTIVE _____

CELEBRITY (MALE) _____

MAD LIBS
EMBRACE THE WEIRD

Uncle Grandpa is not like any other _____. He has
                                          NOUN

a/an _____ mustache and spends his time traveling (the)
          ADJECTIVE

_____ in a tricked-out mobile _____. It doesn't matter
   A PLACE   NOUN

what kind of _____ trouble or adventures he gets into, because he
                  ADJECTIVE

always has his friends around:

- Mr. Gus is a giant green _____ who will _____ help
                                   NOUN   ADVERB

  out Uncle G with anything his _____ desires.
                                  PART OF THE BODY

- Pizza _____ is a/an _____ dude. He's a wiz at
          PERSON IN ROOM (MALE)   ADJECTIVE

  video _____ and likes to eat ice _____ for breakfast.
           PLURAL NOUN   NOUN

- Giant Realistic Flying _____ might be a teenage _____,
                              ANIMAL   NOUN

  but she has a/an _____ bite.
                       ADJECTIVE

- And finally, there's Belly Bag—a bottomless _____ full of
                                                      NOUN

  _____ treats. He always makes sure that _____ has
      ADJECTIVE   CELEBRITY (MALE)

everything that he could ever need.

MAD LIBS® is fun to play with friends, but you can also play it by yourself! To begin with, DO NOT look at the story on the page below. Fill in the blanks on this page with the words called for. Then, using the words you have selected, fill in the blank spaces in the story.

Now you've created your own hilarious MAD LIBS® game!

PIZZA STEVE'S RECIPE FOR SUCCESS

PERSON IN ROOM _____

ADJECTIVE _____

PLURAL NOUN _____

ADJECTIVE _____

ADJECTIVE _____

NOUN _____

NUMBER _____

COLOR _____

ADVERB _____

CELEBRITY _____

ADJECTIVE _____

A PLACE _____

ADJECTIVE _____

'Sup, _____. You want to learn how to be as _____ as me,
         PERSON IN ROOM   ADJECTIVE

Pizza Steve? No problemo. First off, you need some awesome _____.
                                                              PLURAL NOUN

I designed mine myself. They're made out of _____ platinum.
                                              ADJECTIVE

You also need a/an _____ ride. Mine's a totally excellent speed
                    ADJECTIVE

_____—it can go _____ miles an hour. Plus, I'm also
   NOUN   NUMBER

a/an _____ belt in Italian Karate. That's how come I can move so
       COLOR

_____. I don't mean to brag, but I taught _____ how to
   ADVERB   CELEBRITY

fight. And you need to be super musical to be this cooool. I can totally shred it

on my _____ guitar. I'm probably the best guitar player in the entire
       ADJECTIVE

_____. So, yeah, like I was saying . . . Pizza Steve is _____!
   A PLACE   ADJECTIVE

MAD LIBS® is fun to play with friends, but you can also play it by yourself! To begin with, DO NOT look at the story on the page below. Fill in the blanks on this page with the words called for. Then, using the words you have selected, fill in the blank spaces in the story.

Now you've created your own hilarious MAD LIBS® game!

GIANT REALISTIC
FLYING TIGER'S DIARY

NOUN _____

ADJECTIVE _____

ANIMAL _____

PLURAL NOUN _____

PART OF THE BODY _____

VEHICLE _____

PLURAL NOUN _____

PERSON IN ROOM (MALE) _____

A PLACE _____

ADVERB _____

PLURAL NOUN _____

TYPE OF FOOD _____

NOUN _____

MAD LIBS
GIANT REALISTIC
FLYING TIGER'S DIARY

Where does every teen _____ like to hide away her
                          NOUN

super-_____ secrets? In her diary, of course! And Giant Realistic
        ADJECTIVE

Flying _____ is no different. Here are a few snippets:
        ANIMAL

• Pizza Steve always smells like _____. He says that it's his
                                  PLURAL NOUN

  musk, but I think it comes from his _____.
                                       PART OF THE BODY

• Sometimes I like to drive the _____ when everyone is asleep.
                                 VEHICLE

  I like to see how many _____ I can run over before Uncle
                          PLURAL NOUN

  _____ wakes up.
  PERSON IN ROOM (MALE)

• Never take Mr. Gus to (the) _____. He _____ tries
                              A PLACE   ADVERB

  to stomp on all of the _____, and it's really embarrassing.
                          PLURAL NOUN

• I once saw Belly Bag eat _____ right out of the _____.
                           TYPE OF FOOD   NOUN

  Gross.

From UNCLE GRANDPA MAD LIBS® • ™ & © Cartoon Network. (s15). Published in 2015 by Price Stern Sloan,
an imprint of Penguin Random House LLC, 345 Hudson Street, New York, NY 10014.

MAD LIBS® is fun to play with friends, but you can also play it by yourself! To begin with, DO NOT look at the story on the page below. Fill in the blanks on this page with the words called for. Then, using the words you have selected, fill in the blank spaces in the story.

Now you've created your own hilarious MAD LIBS® game!

UNCLE GRANDPA SINGS THE CLASSICS

ADJECTIVE _____

PLURAL NOUN _____

NOUN _____

PART OF THE BODY _____

ADJECTIVE _____

ADJECTIVE _____

NOUN _____

ADJECTIVE _____

VERB _____

ADJECTIVE _____

ADVERB _____

A PLACE _____

PERSON IN ROOM _____

CELEBRITY _____

PLURAL NOUN _____

ADJECTIVE _____

MAD LIBS®
UNCLE GRANDPA SINGS
THE CLASSICS

Here is an excerpt from the liner notes of the _____ collection of all
                                                    ADJECTIVE

of Uncle Grandpa's hit songs, *Uncle Grandpa Sings the* _____:
                                                              PLURAL NOUN

Interdimensional super-_____ Uncle Grandpa is not
                              NOUN

just a pretty _____, he's also a/an _____
                PART OF THE BODY   ADJECTIVE

vocal performer. Many of his _____ hits can be
                                    ADJECTIVE

heard on this album. Some of the tracks included are: "Diggin'

a/an _____," "Mr. Gus Is _____," "Don't
          NOUN   ADJECTIVE

_____ Pizza Steve," and "_____ on a Boat."
     VERB   ADJECTIVE

Uncle Grandpa can sing as _____ as any of the greatest
                                 ADVERB

vocalists in (the) _____, including _____ and
                      A PLACE   PERSON IN ROOM

_____. Some have gone so far as to describe his voice as
   CELEBRITY

sounding like _____ blowing in a/an _____
                 PLURAL NOUN   ADJECTIVE

summer breeze.

MAD LIBS® is fun to play with friends, but you can also play it by yourself! To begin with, DO NOT look at the story on the page below. Fill in the blanks on this page with the words called for. Then, using the words you have selected, fill in the blank spaces in the story.

Now you've created your own hilarious MAD LIBS® game!

BEING UNCLE GRANDPA

PART OF THE BODY _____

PLURAL NOUN _____

NOUN _____

ADVERB _____

ADJECTIVE _____

NOUN _____

ADJECTIVE _____

PLURAL NOUN _____

ADJECTIVE _____

ADVERB _____

ADJECTIVE _____

NOUN _____

PLURAL NOUN _____

ADJECTIVE _____

MAD LIBS®
BEING UNCLE GRANDPA

What would you do if Uncle Grandpa got his _____ stuck
                                              PART OF THE BODY

in a jar of _____ and you had to take over for him? Not just any
            PLURAL NOUN

_____ could do the job as _____ as Uncle Grandpa. It takes
    NOUN   ADVERB

more than a pair of _____ suspenders and a cool _____
                       ADJECTIVE   NOUN

to fill his shoes. If you're filling in for Uncle Grandpa, there are a few

_____ things to know. First off, you must always remain positive
   ADJECTIVE

in the face of _____—no matter how _____ they seem.
                PLURAL NOUN   ADJECTIVE

Second, you must approach everything as _____ as a child because
                                             ADVERB

children always know the _____ way to do things. Finally, and
                              ADJECTIVE

this is the most important _____, always make sure to have your
                                NOUN

_____ with you. If all else fails, just remember that the best way to
   PLURAL NOUN

do something is often the most _____ way.
                                   ADJECTIVE

MAD LIBS® is fun to play with friends, but you can also play it by yourself! To begin with, DO NOT look at the story on the page below. Fill in the blanks on this page with the words called for. Then, using the words you have selected, fill in the blank spaces in the story.

Now you've created your own hilarious MAD LIBS® game!

WHAT'S IN UNCLE GRANDPA'S BELLY BAG?

ADJECTIVE _____

COLOR _____

NOUN _____

ADJECTIVE _____

NOUN _____

NOUN _____

PLURAL NOUN _____

ADVERB _____

A PLACE _____

NOUN _____

VERB _____

NUMBER _____

ADVERB _____

PART OF THE BODY _____

One of Uncle Grandpa's _____ friends is his bright _____
_____ADJECTIVE_____COLOR

Belly _____. Belly Bag is a/an _____ creature full of
_____NOUN_____ADJECTIVE

every kind of _____ that Uncle Grandpa could ever ask for. If Uncle
_____NOUN

Grandpa ever found himself stuck on an inescapable _____,
_____NOUN

all he'd have to do is ask and he'd be handed a jar of _____ that
_____PLURAL NOUN

could _____ create a door back to (the) _____. Or Belly
_____ADVERB_____A PLACE

Bag could give him a magical _____ that would allow him to
_____NOUN

_____ to another dimension. Over the years, Belly Bag has helped
____VERB

Uncle Grandpa out of at least _____ jams, and that's why Uncle G
_____NUMBER

never leaves the RV without Belly Bag strapped _____ around his
_____ADVERB

_____!
___PART OF THE BODY

From UNCLE GRANDPA MAD LIBS® • ™ & © Cartoon Network. (s15). Published in 2015 by Price Stern Sloan,
an imprint of Penguin Random House LLC, 345 Hudson Street, New York, NY 10014.

MAD LIBS® is fun to play with friends, but you can also play it by yourself! To begin with, DO NOT look at the story on the page below. Fill in the blanks on this page with the words called for. Then, using the words you have selected, fill in the blank spaces in the story.

Now you've created your own hilarious MAD LIBS® game!

THE JOY OF TINY MIRACLE

NOUN _____

ADJECTIVE _____

NOUN _____

NUMBER _____

PART OF THE BODY (PLURAL) _____

PLURAL NOUN _____

NOUN _____

PLURAL NOUN _____

ARTICLE OF CLOTHING _____

COLOR _____

PLURAL NOUN _____

VERB _____

NOUN _____

NOUN _____

VERB _____

NOUN _____

MAD LIBS®
THE JOY OF TINY MIRACLE

Whenever there's a/an _____ on the RV, Uncle Grandpa knows that
                      NOUN

he can call on _____ Miracle for help—no problem! Tiny Miracle is
                ADJECTIVE

an amazing robot _____ with _____ legs and extendable
                  NOUN   NUMBER

_____ with _____ on the end. They make it easy for
PART OF THE BODY (PLURAL)   PLURAL NOUN

him to reach the top of the _____ or retrieve _____ that are
                             NOUN   PLURAL NOUN

trapped inside the toilet. Tiny Miracle always wears a red _____
                                                           ARTICLE OF CLOTHING

and a/an _____ T-shirt that reads: I ♡_____. And whenever
          COLOR   PLURAL NOUN

he shows up, he says, "Did someone _____ Tiny Miracle?" He can
                                    VERB

clean up _____ stains on the walls, rewire a/an _____, or
          NOUN   NOUN

even _____ an amazing ice-cream _____.
      VERB   NOUN

From UNCLE GRANDPA MAD LIBS® • ™ & © Cartoon Network. (s15). Published in 2015 by Price Stern Sloan,
an imprint of Penguin Random House LLC, 345 Hudson Street, New York, NY 10014.

MAD LIBS® is fun to play with friends, but you can also play it by yourself! To begin with, DO NOT look at the story on the page below. Fill in the blanks on this page with the words called for. Then, using the words you have selected, fill in the blank spaces in the story.

Now you've created your own hilarious MAD LIBS® game!

MAP OF THE UG-RV

ADJECTIVE _____

PLURAL NOUN _____

NOUN _____

NUMBER _____

ADJECTIVE _____

ADJECTIVE _____

PLURAL NOUN _____

NOUN _____

ADJECTIVE _____

PLURAL NOUN _____

NOUN _____

ADVERB _____

NOUN _____

PLURAL NOUN _____

EXCLAMATION _____

ADJECTIVE _____

MAD LIBS
MAP OF THE UG-RV

Uncle Grandpa's RV is one _____ place. It might seem like all the
____ADJECTIVE____

_____ wouldn't fit inside one mobile _____, but there
__PLURAL NOUN__   __NOUN__

are actually more than _____ rooms inside the _____
                          __NUMBER__   __ADJECTIVE__

RV! Pizza Steve's room is super-double _____ and is filled with all
                                          __ADJECTIVE__

different types of one-of-a-kind _____ that he invented himself. Giant
                                    __PLURAL NOUN__

Realistic Flying Tiger's room is a totally normal teenage _____'s
                                                             __NOUN__

room. There are posters of _____ boy bands, and everything is
                              __ADJECTIVE__

covered with pink _____. Uncle G's room has a bed shaped like a
                     __PLURAL NOUN__

racing _____ and weapons hung _____ on all the walls.
          __NOUN__   __ADVERB__

Mr. Gus's room has a/an _____ hanging from the ceiling, and there
                           __NOUN__

are heavy _____ and other exercise equipment scattered around.
             __PLURAL NOUN__

_____—all of this inside one _____ place!
__EXCLAMATION__   __ADJECTIVE__

MAD LIBS® is fun to play with friends, but you can also play it by yourself! To begin with, DO NOT look at the story on the page below. Fill in the blanks on this page with the words called for. Then, using the words you have selected, fill in the blank spaces in the story.

Now you've created your own hilarious MAD LIBS® game!

UNCLE GRANDPA'S FAVORITE ADVENTURES

ADJECTIVE _____

NOUN _____

NOUN _____

PLURAL NOUN _____

ADJECTIVE _____

ADVERB _____

TYPE OF LIQUID _____

ADJECTIVE _____

PERSON IN ROOM _____

ADJECTIVE _____

NOUN _____

MAD LIBS®
UNCLE GRANDPA'S
FAVORITE ADVENTURES

Oh boy, Uncle Grandpa and the gang sure have had a lot of _____

___ADJECTIVE___

adventures. There was the one time that they tried to pick a/an _____

___NOUN___

in the desert, but it turned out to be a/an _____ from outer space!

___NOUN___

Luckily, Mr. Gus showed up in a tight pair of _____ and saved the day.

___PLURAL NOUN___

Another time, Uncle Grandpa and the gang had to battle a/an _____

___ADJECTIVE___

Mustache Monster. They had to work _____ to cover it in mustache

___ADVERB___

_____ before it destroyed the RV. And then there was the time Uncle

___TYPE OF LIQUID___

Grandpa had to travel to a/an _____ dimension and battle an evil

___ADJECTIVE___

version of himself called Emperor _____. Wow, those are some

___PERSON IN ROOM___

_____ adventures. And that only scratches the _____ of it!

___ADJECTIVE___   ___NOUN___

MAD LIBS® is fun to play with friends, but you can also play it by yourself! To begin with, DO NOT look at the story on the page below. Fill in the blanks on this page with the words called for. Then, using the words you have selected, fill in the blank spaces in the story.

Now you've created your own hilarious MAD LIBS® game!

MR. GUS TELLS IT LIKE IT IS

PERSON IN ROOM _____

ADJECTIVE _____

NUMBER _____

PERSON IN ROOM _____

ADJECTIVE _____

NOUN _____

ADVERB _____

NOUN _____

PLURAL NOUN _____

VERB _____

ARTICLE OF CLOTHING _____

NUMBER _____

COLOR _____

VERB _____

NOUN _____

PART OF THE BODY _____

MAD LIBS

MR. GUS TELLS IT LIKE IT IS

Not every problem needs Uncle _____ to solve it. Sometimes all
                                   PERSON IN ROOM

you need is a/an _____ green dinosaur to set things right. Mr.
                    ADJECTIVE

Gus has _____ rules for solving problems. The first rule is that
             NUMBER

Pizza _____ is always wrong. You should always do the opposite
         PERSON IN ROOM

of what that _____ slice of _____ and cheese says.
                 ADJECTIVE   NOUN

Second, always proceed _____. You can never tell what will be on
                            ADVERB

the other side of a/an _____ or inside a jar of _____.
                           NOUN   PLURAL NOUN

Third, always _____ in style. It's important to wear your favorite
                   VERB

_____. Mr. Gus's favorite thing to wear is a/an _____
ARTICLE OF CLOTHING   NUMBER

-year-old pair of _____ jorts. It doesn't matter if you think people
                      COLOR

will _____ at you—your outfit just might save the _____.
         VERB   NOUN

Lastly, if something doesn't go your way—you can always crush it under your

massive _____.
           PART OF THE BODY

MAD LIBS® is fun to play with friends, but you can also play it by yourself! To begin with, DO NOT look at the story on the page below. Fill in the blanks on this page with the words called for. Then, using the words you have selected, fill in the blank spaces in the story.

Now you've created your own hilarious MAD LIBS® game!

UNCLE GRANDPA SAVES THE DAY

PERSON IN ROOM _____

ADJECTIVE _____

NOUN _____

CELEBRITY _____

NOUN _____

NOUN _____

PLURAL NOUN _____

NOUN _____

NUMBER _____

A PLACE _____

NOUN _____

NOUN _____

PLURAL NOUN _____

NOUN _____

"Okay, _____, all aboard the UG-RV," said Uncle Grandpa as he
PERSON IN ROOM

raced across the _____ ground and toward the grassy _____
ADJECTIVE   NOUN

where the RV was parked. "Where are we going, Uncle Grandpa?" asked

Mr. _____. "We haven't found the missing _____ yet."
CELEBRITY   NOUN

"Why were we looking for that again?" Uncle Grandpa asked as he entered

the UG-RV's _____. "Because," replied Pizza Steve, "you said we
NOUN

needed to bring it to the king of the _____ so he'll release the golden
PLURAL NOUN

_____ before the clock strikes _____." "Oh, right," said
NOUN   NUMBER

Uncle Grandpa. "Quick! Let's get to (the) _____, Uncle Grandpa.
A PLACE

Full _____ ahead!" "You got it," answered a second Uncle Grandpa
NOUN

seated at the RV's _____. "But, Uncle Grandpa," Belly Bag pleaded,
NOUN

"the UG-RV's stuck in a puddle of _____. We'll never get out of
PLURAL NOUN

here." "Don't be so sure," both Uncle Grandpas replied at once as they pressed

the _____ button on the dashboard.
NOUN

MAD LIBS® is fun to play with friends, but you can also play it by yourself! To begin with, DO NOT look at the story on the page below. Fill in the blanks on this page with the words called for. Then, using the words you have selected, fill in the blank spaces in the story.

Now you've created your own hilarious MAD LIBS® game!

UNCLE GRANDPA THROUGH HISTORY

NOUN _____

PLURAL NOUN _____

VERB _____

ADJECTIVE _____

PERSON IN ROOM (FEMALE) _____

NOUN _____

A PLACE _____

PLURAL NOUN _____

NOUN _____

PLURAL NOUN _____

NUMBER _____

PLURAL NOUN _____

PERSON IN ROOM _____

PLURAL NOUN _____

If there's one thing that Uncle Grandpa knows a/an _____ or two
                                                          NOUN

about, it's _____. So it's a good thing that he can _____
            PLURAL NOUN   VERB

through time. Once he needed to help a/an _____ girl named
                                              ADJECTIVE

_____ find her missing _____. Uncle Grandpa
PERSON IN ROOM (FEMALE)   NOUN

knew exactly where to look—the ancient _____. Another time he
                                              A PLACE

had to defeat an army of hungry _____ that were eating their way
                                     PLURAL NOUN

through the _____ Empire. Luckily, he remembered to bring along a
                 NOUN

bag of delicious _____. Uncle G doesn't just travel through history—
                    PLURAL NOUN

sometimes he brings it to him, like the time he invited _____
                                                              NUMBER

prehistoric _____ to little _____'s birthday party, and
                PLURAL NOUN   PERSON IN ROOM

they ate all the _____.
                    PLURAL NOUN

MAD LIBS® is fun to play with friends, but you can also play it by yourself! To begin with, DO NOT look at the story on the page below. Fill in the blanks on this page with the words called for. Then, using the words you have selected, fill in the blank spaces in the story.

Now you've created your own hilarious MAD LIBS® game!

BALLAD OF THE UG-RV

ADJECTIVE _____

PLURAL NOUN _____

PERSON IN ROOM (MALE) _____

CELEBRITY _____

ADJECTIVE _____

VERB _____

A PLACE _____

NOUN _____

VERB ENDING IN "ING" _____

PLURAL NOUN _____

ADVERB _____

PLURAL NOUN _____

PLURAL NOUN _____

NUMBER _____

ADJECTIVE _____

ADJECTIVE _____

MAD LIBS®
BALLAD OF THE UG-RV

Oh, Uncle Grandpa has a/an _____ mobile home.
ADJECTIVE

It takes him and his _____ everywhere they want to roam.
PLURAL NOUN

With his pals Mr. _____, Belly Bag, _____, and
PERSON IN ROOM (MALE)   CELEBRITY

Pizza Steve,

Even a/an _____ Realistic Flying Tiger would never want
ADJECTIVE

to _____.
VERB

From the kitchen to (the) _____ to the _____ room,
A PLACE   NOUN

Uncle Grandpa likes to go "vroom, vroom."

When he's _____ in his UG-RV,
VERB ENDING IN "ING"

And helping _____ and doing it _____,
PLURAL NOUN   ADVERB

From the deepest depths of the _____,
PLURAL NOUN

With its four _____ always in motion,
PLURAL NOUN

To _____ miles up an old _____ tree,
NUMBER   ADJECTIVE

Nothing can stop Uncle G's _____ UG-RV.
ADJECTIVE

MAD LIBS® is fun to play with friends, but you can also play it by yourself! To begin with, DO NOT look at the story on the page below. Fill in the blanks on this page with the words called for. Then, using the words you have selected, fill in the blank spaces in the story.

Now you've created your own hilarious MAD LIBS® game!

GOOD MORNING

PLURAL NOUN _____

ADJECTIVE _____

PLURAL NOUN _____

VERB _____

PLURAL NOUN _____

A PLACE _____

PLURAL NOUN _____

ADJECTIVE _____

PERSON IN ROOM (MALE) _____

NOUN _____

VERB _____

PLURAL NOUN _____

CELEBRITY _____

A PLACE _____

It's always a good morning for Uncle Grandpa . . . Here's why:

- You know it's a good morning when Mr. Gus makes _____
  PLURAL NOUN

  for breakfast—even if Pizza Steve pours _____ sauce all over it.
  ADJECTIVE

- You know it's a good morning when there are no _____ hiding
  PLURAL NOUN

  under the bed. They always try to _____ all of Giant Realistic
  VERB

  Flying Tiger's favorite _____!
  PLURAL NOUN

- You know it's a good morning when Uncle Grandpa takes everyone to

  (the) _____ and buys them all _____. Pizza Steve
  A PLACE   PLURAL NOUN

  always gets a/an _____ one!
  ADJECTIVE

- You know it's a good morning when _____ needs
  PERSON IN ROOM (MALE)

  Uncle Grandpa's help finding his missing _____.
  NOUN

- You know it's a good morning when Belly Bag and Mr. Gus

  _____ their way through a whole bag of sugar _____
  VERB   PLURAL NOUN

  before taking _____ for a walk to (the) _____.
  CELEBRITY   A PLACE

MAD LIBS® is fun to play with friends, but you can also play it by yourself! To begin with, DO NOT look at the story on the page below. Fill in the blanks on this page with the words called for. Then, using the words you have selected, fill in the blank spaces in the story.

Now you've created your own hilarious MAD LIBS® game!

ODE TO MR. GUS

NOUN _____

ADJECTIVE _____

ADJECTIVE _____

PLURAL NOUN _____

NUMBER _____

PLURAL NOUN _____

ADJECTIVE _____

PERSON IN ROOM _____

NOUN _____

PLURAL NOUN _____

PLURAL NOUN _____

PART OF THE BODY (PLURAL) _____

ADVERB _____

PLURAL NOUN _____

MAD LIBS®
ODE TO MR. GUS

Mr. Gus might seem like a sour _____, but there are reasons why

NOUN

Uncle Grandpa likes having the _____ dinosaur around. First off,

ADJECTIVE

Mr. Gus is super _____. He can open a jar of _____

ADJECTIVE · PLURAL NOUN

without any help, and he lifts _____ pounds of _____

NUMBER · PLURAL NOUN

every morning! But he's more than just brawn; he also has a/an _____

ADJECTIVE

side and often acts nicely toward _____. He can be like a big cuddly

PERSON IN ROOM

_____. But it's not all fun and _____, especially when

NOUN · PLURAL NOUN

Pizza Steve is around. That guy is always making up _____, and it

PLURAL NOUN

really gets on Mr. Gus's _____. Sometimes, to relieve the

PART OF THE BODY (PLURAL)

stress, Mr. Gus will _____ stomp all over _____.

ADVERB · PLURAL NOUN

MAD LIBS® is fun to play with friends, but you can also play it by yourself! To begin with, DO NOT look at the story on the page below. Fill in the blanks on this page with the words called for. Then, using the words you have selected, fill in the blank spaces in the story.

Now you've created your own hilarious MAD LIBS® game!

NEW EXPERIENCES

PERSON IN ROOM _____

PLURAL NOUN _____

ADJECTIVE _____

VERB _____

PLURAL NOUN _____

NOUN _____

ADJECTIVE _____

PLURAL NOUN _____

ADJECTIVE _____

PLURAL NOUN _____

ADVERB _____

ADJECTIVE _____

Beary Nice: Hey, Hot Dog _____, ready for some new
<u>PERSON IN ROOM</u>

_____?
<u>PLURAL NOUN</u>

Hot Dog Person: I don't know, Beary. It could be _____.
<u>ADJECTIVE</u>

Beary Nice: Guess what we're going to _____ today?
<u>VERB</u>

Hot Dog Person: Shop for _____?
<u>PLURAL NOUN</u>

Beary Nice: No, we could try our very first _____. Aren't you
<u>NOUN</u>

excited?

Hot Dog Person: I don't know. It could be _____.
<u>ADJECTIVE</u>

Beary Nice: But it could also be delicious. That's why we have new

_____.
<u>PLURAL NOUN</u>

Hot Dog Person: That's a possibility. But it also could be _____.
<u>ADJECTIVE</u>

Beary Nice: How about we use our _____ to come up with a new
<u>PLURAL NOUN</u>

experience?

Hot Dog Person: What if I don't have one of those?

Beary Nice: That's okay, you can _____ share mine!
<u>ADVERB</u>

Hot Dog Person: Okay. I'll give it a try.

Beary Nice: That sounds Beary _____. Oh wait, that's me!
<u>ADJECTIVE</u>

MAD LIBS® is fun to play with friends, but you can also play it by yourself! To begin with, DO NOT look at the story on the page below. Fill in the blanks on this page with the words called for. Then, using the words you have selected, fill in the blank spaces in the story.

Now you've created your own hilarious MAD LIBS® game!

MEET AUNT GRANDMA

NOUN _____

PERSON IN ROOM (FEMALE) _____

NOUN _____

PLURAL NOUN _____

ADJECTIVE _____

PLURAL NOUN _____

NOUN _____

ADVERB _____

ADJECTIVE _____

ADJECTIVE _____

A PLACE _____

NOUN _____

NOUN _____

PLURAL NOUN _____

MAD LIBS
MEET AUNT GRANDMA

Beautiful _____, as I always say. That's right, I'm Aunt
　　　　　　 NOUN

_____. I'm everyone's practical _____ and
PERSON IN ROOM (FEMALE)　　　　　　　　　　　　　　NOUN

grandmother. Much like Uncle Grandpa, I help kids with their _____.
　　　　　　　　　　　　　　　　　　　　　　　　　　　　　PLURAL NOUN

Except that I am faster, smarter, and let's face it, way more _____
　　　　　　　　　　　　　　　　　　　　　　　　　　　　ADJECTIVE

than Uncle Grandpa. I know exactly what _____ want. If they want
　　　　　　　　　　　　　　　　　　　PLURAL NOUN

a new _____ or if they need help with their homework, I give it
　　　　　NOUN

to them _____ without dragging them on some _____
　　　　　ADVERB　　　　　　　　　　　　　　　　　　　　ADJECTIVE

adventure. I believe that _____ problems require simple solutions.
　　　　　　　　　　　　　ADJECTIVE

Uncle Grandpa likes to put on a show. He'll take kids to (the) _____
　　　　　　　　　　　　　　　　　　　　　　　　　　　　　A PLACE

to teach them how to play an electric _____ or ruin their papier-
　　　　　　　　　　　　　　　　　　　NOUN

mâché _____ they worked so hard on for the school science fair. But
　　　　NOUN

I'll show him: _____ do not solve problems—Aunt Grandma does!
　　　　　　　PLURAL NOUN

From UNCLE GRANDPA MAD LIBS® • ™ & © Cartoon Network. (s15). Published in 2015 by Price Stern Sloan,
an imprint of Penguin Random House LLC, 345 Hudson Street, New York, NY 10014.

MAD LIBS® is fun to play with friends, but you can also play it by yourself! To begin with, DO NOT look at the story on the page below. Fill in the blanks on this page with the words called for. Then, using the words you have selected, fill in the blank spaces in the story.

Now you've created your own hilarious MAD LIBS® game!

SLICE OF LIFE WITH PIZZA STEVE

PERSON IN ROOM _____

ADJECTIVE _____

NOUN _____

ADJECTIVE _____

VERB ENDING IN "ING" _____

ADJECTIVE _____

ADVERB _____

NOUN _____

CELEBRITY _____

ADJECTIVE _____

PLURAL NOUN _____

VERB ENDING IN "ING" _____

NOUN _____

PLURAL NOUN _____

'Sup, Broasaurus-_____. I'm Pizza Steve and I'm a/an
          PERSON IN ROOM

_____ dude. Me and my best _____, Mr. Gus, love to
    ADJECTIVE   NOUN

go on _____ adventures together. The best thing is that we both
        ADJECTIVE

dig _____ out to some _____ jams. Mr. G will
    VERB ENDING IN "ING"   ADJECTIVE

_____ listen to any _____ that I put on the old car radio.
    ADVERB   NOUN

And he loves it when my friends come to visit. Mr. Gus just can't get enough of

Pizza _____; they always make a lot of _____ noise with
        CELEBRITY   ADJECTIVE

their electric _____. Sometimes we just sit around the RV and take
            PLURAL NOUN

turns _____ my thick, luxurious _____. Yeah,
    VERB ENDING IN "ING"   NOUN

you could say Mr. Gus and me are like two _____ in a pod.
                                        PLURAL NOUN

From UNCLE GRANDPA MAD LIBS® • ™ & © Cartoon Network. (s15). Published in 2015 by Price Stern Sloan,
an imprint of Penguin Random House LLC, 345 Hudson Street, New York, NY 10014.

MAD LIBS® is fun to play with friends, but you can also play it by yourself! To begin with, DO NOT look at the story on the page below. Fill in the blanks on this page with the words called for. Then, using the words you have selected, fill in the blank spaces in the story.

Now you've created your own hilarious MAD LIBS® game!

HOW MANY UNCLE GRANDPAS DOES IT TAKE TO SCREW IN A LIGHTBULB?

ADJECTIVE _____

NOUN _____

VERB (PAST TENSE) _____

PERSON IN ROOM _____

NOUN _____

NOUN _____

PART OF THE BODY _____

A PLACE _____

NUMBER _____

COLOR _____

NOUN _____

NUMBER _____

PLURAL NOUN _____

CELEBRITY _____

MAD LIBS®
GIANT REALISTIC FLYING
TIGER'S TIPS FOR TEENS

Giant _____ Flying Tiger knows everything there is about being a
          ADJECTIVE

teenage _____. Here's her advice for all wannabe _____:
          NOUN   PLURAL NOUN

• All teens should have a crush on pop star _____. Not
                                            PERSON IN ROOM (MALE)

  only is he a/an _____ singer, he also has a beautiful
                   ADJECTIVE

  _____.
   PART OF THE BODY

• It's important to take care of your _____. That's why I go to
                                       PLURAL NOUN

  the salon _____ times a week. And of course _____
             NUMBER   PERSON IN ROOM

  pays for it.

• Shopping is crucial—every girl needs a/an _____ coat. Mine
                                             ADJECTIVE

  has _____ and black stripes, and it covers my whole body.
       COLOR

  And _____—you can never have too many.
       ARTICLE OF CLOTHING (PLURAL)

• It's important to like _____ things, like ponies, princesses,
                         COLOR

  and _____.
       PLURAL NOUN

From UNCLE GRANDPA MAD LIBS® • ™ & © Cartoon Network. (s15). Published in 2015 by Price Stern Sloan,
an imprint of Penguin Random House LLC, 345 Hudson Street, New York, NY 10014.

MAD LIBS® is fun to play with friends, but you can also play it by yourself! To begin with, DO NOT look at the story on the page below. Fill in the blanks on this page with the words called for. Then, using the words you have selected, fill in the blank spaces in the story.

Now you've created your own hilarious MAD LIBS® game!

BELLY BAG'S CLOSING WORDS

PLURAL NOUN _____

NOUN _____

ADVERB _____

ADJECTIVE _____

CELEBRITY _____

ADJECTIVE _____

VERB (PAST TENSE) _____

PLURAL NOUN _____

ADJECTIVE _____

PLURAL NOUN _____

A PLACE _____

NUMBER _____

ADJECTIVE _____

COLOR _____

PART OF THE BODY _____

NOUN _____

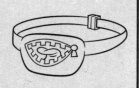
Hi, Uncle Grandpa's _____. Thanks for spending some time with us.
PLURAL NOUN

I didn't think we'd get to the end of the _____ so _____.
NOUN   ADVERB

You must be very _____. Well, we've found out a lot about Mr.
ADJECTIVE

Gus, Pizza Steve, _____, and all of Uncle Grandpa's friends. Oh
CELEBRITY

boy, this has been one _____ adventure. And we _____
ADJECTIVE   VERB (PAST TENSE)

lots of new things. You know, I never knew that I liked _____ so
PLURAL NOUN

much or that Giant Realistic Flying Tiger had such a/an _____
ADJECTIVE

collection of _____. I can't remember the last time I had so much
PLURAL NOUN

fun—maybe it was that time Uncle Grandpa took me to (the) _____
A PLACE

for my birthday. I ate _____ pieces of cake. But this book is better
NUMBER

than cake. It has stories about _____ heroes, a big _____
ADJECTIVE   COLOR

dinosaur in jorts, and a handsome _____ Bag. So, as Uncle
PART OF THE BODY

Grandpa always says, embrace the _____.
NOUN